Norwegian Patterns for Knitting

Mette N. Handberg

Norwegian Patterns for Knitting

Classic Sweaters, Hats, Vests, and Mittens

TRAFALGAR SQUARE
North Pomfret, Vermont

First published in the United States of America
in 2010 by
Trafalgar Square Books
North Pomfret, Vermont 05053

Originally published in Norwegian as Maske for
Maske by J.W. Cappelens Forlag as

© 2001 J.W. Cappelens Forlag as
English translation © 2010 Trafalgar Square Books

ISBN: 978-1-57076-448-6

Library of Congress Control Number: 2010924148

Translation by Carol Huebscher Rhoades
Photography: Grethe Syvertsen Arnstad
Styling: Susanne Wilnersson
Pattern Digitalization: Vivian Høxbro
Graphic Design: Unni Dahl
Reproduction: Capella

Garments knitted by Ingrid Loennechen Jentoft,
Ingeborg Rinnan, Eli Fyhn, Randi Brechan, and
Mette N. Handberg

Clothing worn by the models provided by Night,
H&M, Cubus, Benetton, In Wear, Matinique, Fru
Lyng and Bianco.

Printed in China

Table of Contents

Preface

There was once a time when everyone knew how to knit and almost every Norwegian practiced that skill. We learned the art when we were quite young. For many it was little more than a duty but for most of us it was a given that knitting meant great pleasure and enjoyment. Time was used well. Knitting needles clicked in the classroom and at lectures, irritating to some but an expression of enthusiasm for many more. Now the ardent knitting of the 60s and 70s has almost disappeared. This most Norwegian of skills is no longer taught in schools and as long as young mothers barely master these "obvious" skills it will continue that way. The time when little girls made their first fumbling attempts and sighed at the long pointy needles seems to have vanished.

"Norwegian lice sweaters" is an internationally recognized concept. Our pattern traditions go a long way back in history even if they weren't, as we believe, created in this country. The most typical example of the so-called "eight petal rose" can be found in a number of cultures. However, we have clearly made it "the most Norwegian of the Norwegian" and along with the "lice" and other beautiful patterns, we have a tradition to be proud of and well worth building upon. Maybe just when knitting is no longer part of people's everyday lives is precisely when it can become most cherished? Our identity as a knitting culture always invokes admiration.

To reawaken interest in Norwegian knitting, we cannot simply push the same ideas again and again. Designers crave change and renewal and customers want more than just the "Norwegian" and traditional. In this book you'll find not just lice sweaters with moose and roses, but also garments for work, everyday wear, and parties, for children and adults. Use the book wisely: take notes and fill the margins of the book with your notes and records—that's what they are meant for!

Mette N. Handberg

Coffee Bean

Techniques

—with many clever and useful tips for anyone who wants to knit with the best possible results.

Gauge

Always start your project with a gauge swatch, worked in a single color and in pattern. Cast on 12 stitches and work for a couple of inches or a few centimeters and then measure the gauge over 10 sts. Use smaller needles or knit more tightly on single-color rows or sections. You need to try out various needle sizes.

Alfa:	10 sts x approx 13 rows = 4 x 4 in / 10 x 10 cm.
Peer Gynt:	22 sts and approx 27 rows = 4 x 4 in / 10 x 10 cm.
Smart:	24 sts x approx 29 rows = 4 x 4 in / 10 x 10 cm.
Smart Tweed:	22 sts x approx 27 rows = 4 x 4 in / 10 x 10 cm.
Telemark:	25 sts x approx 29-30 rows = 4 x 4 in / 10 x 10 cm.
Sisu:	27 sts x approx 31-32 rows = 4 x 4 in / 10 x 10 cm.
Mandarin Classic:	22 sts x approx 27-28 rows = 4 x 4 in / 10 x 10 cm.

In a single-color section, there will often be a few more rows (as many as 4 rows) than for the pattern gauge. It is clearly indicated whenever gauge changes within a pattern.

Recommended Needle Sizes

Alfa:	US 10, 10 ½, 11 / 6, 6.5, or 7 mm
Peer Gynt:	US 4-6 / 3.5-4 mm. I usually knit with a US 4 / 3.5 mm for the patterning with this yarn and with US 2 / 3 mm for the single-color sections.
Smart:	US 4-6 / 3.5-4 mm (I prefer US 2-4 / 3-3.5 mm needles for this yarn).
Telemark:	US 2 / 3 mm.
Sisu:	US 2 / 3mm. It is possible to use a US 4 / 3.5 mm for pattern knitting if you knit a bit tightly. The yarn is somewhat elastic. Check gauge carefully.

Mandarin Classic:	US 2 or 4 / 3 or 3.5 mm.

Needle sizes are recommendations only. It is very important to use the size needles that give you the correct gauge. In this book, linings and facings are often worked with the same size needles but fewer stitches as for body of garment.

Yarn Substitution

It is always best to use the yarn recommended in the pattern. However, if that is not possible, choose a substitute yarn that is as close as possible in grist (relation of yardage to weight) and texture. For example, if the suggested yarn is a smooth wool with 100 yards in 50 g, then another smooth wool yarn with 90-110 yards per 50 g can be usually be substituted successfully. Make a 4 x 4 in / 10 x 10 cm (or larger) gauge swatch to be sure substituted yarn will work.

Alfa:	85% wool/15% mohair superwash, 66 yds / 60 m per 50 g
Peer Gynt:	100% wool, 98 yds / 91 m per 50 g
Smart and Smart Tweed:	100% superwash wool, 110 yds / 100 m per 50 g
Telemark:	100% wool, 153 yds / 140 m per 50 g (note: Telemark is no longer available)

1

| Sisu: | 80% wool, 20% nylon, 215 yds / 160 m per 50 g |
| Mandarin Classic: | 100% mercerized cotton, 120 yds / 110 m per 50 g |

Casting On

Use a knit cast-on, working a little tightly. This cast-on makes an elastic and even edge and it is easy to pick up stitches from it later if necessary.

Increasing

Use make 1 (m1) for increases: lift the strand between two stitches and knit into back loop (to avoid holes). If the row below is worked in a contrast color and the increase will be noticeable, tighten the working yarn a bit on each increase. Knit at least 1 row in a single-color before increasing. Unless otherwise specified, increase with m1 on the right side (RS) of garment.

In some cases, it is better to increase by working into the front and back of the same stitch (k1f&b). This shows as a purl stitch and is the best method for increasing on the wrong side. It is also the best increase to use when knitting with dark yarn. For example, it makes it easier to see sleeve increases.

In most of the patterns, increases are worked before the fold line. Facings should be knit somewhat tightly so they won't be too wide. This is explained in individual patterns.

Picking up and Knitting Stitches

Never pick up stitches directly from the knitting!
Use a crochet hook. Hold the hook as for a knitting needle. With RS facing, use a new strand of yarn to pick up and knit stitches. Slide the sts down the hook and then onto a knitting needle. I actually hold the knitting needle as if it were a crochet hook and twist the stitches for the correct mount for knitting when transferring to another needle.

Sometimes you will pick up the stitches directly from the cast-on row. In this case, do not use a new strand of yarn. Pick up the stitches through the small "beads" of the cast-on row and then knit into these sts. The knit cast-on is elastic and doesn't tighten up.

Counting Stitches

1, 2, 3, 4 – this is silly!
2, 4, 6, 8 – this is a little easier.
You can eyeball a certain number without actually counting them. We can easily discern 5 stitches without counting them and this makes the whole operation quicker and more reliable. "See" 5 sts and move your fingers over them. If you make a habit of this method,

you can count around a long circular needle without any effort and without needing total silence around you.

Stranding the Yarn over a Long Stretch

Always catch the unused strand of yarn in two-color knitting after every 3rd st. If the garment has a facing, you can strand over more stitches although never more than 5. Stagger catches so they are not stacked above each other. For adult garments, you could work 4 stitches without catching the strands.

Knots in the Yarn

Cut the yarn, preferably at the "steek" or the side. A single-color sweater will not look good with the yarn spliced at the middle of the stomach.

Ripping

Sometimes it is best to rip out. Insert a smaller needle across the row you have to rip back to and then rip back.

Binding Off

Knit 2 sts, *slip the first st over the 2nd st, k1 and repeat from *. This method of decreasing can easily pull the fabric in so use it only over small sections.

Sleeve Top Finishing (stretchy bind-off)

Knit 2 sts together, slip the st back onto left needle. Knit 2 sts tog, slip the st to left needle, and repeat.

Three-Needle Bind-Off (Joining Shoulders)

This method makes a stable and firm finishing for the shoulders.

With each set of shoulder sts on a separate needle, hold needles so that RS faces RS. Knit together the first st from each needle and repeat with the second st on each needle. Now there are 2 sts on right needle. Slip the first st on right needle over the next one so 1 st remains. Knit 2 sts together from left needles and slip right needle st over it, etc.

A little relief st stripe shows on the WS and it will look as if 1 stitch has been sewn into each stitch on the RS

For pattern knitting, make sure that the pattern matches on both sides.

Buttonholes

Usually we bind off 3 sts for each buttonhole. When the last st has been bound off, there will be a little strand diagonally over the next st. To avoid this: bind off the first 2 sts. Knit the next st and move the last 2 sts to left needle; bind off the innermost st over the outermost, move sts back to right needle, tighten yarn, and continue.

This technique is also useful for binding off at a split neck.

Instead of casting on 3 new sts, you could make 3 half hitches, especially when using thick yarn. With this simpler method, you avoid turning the work, especially when there are many stitches to cast-on. Do not bind off too tightly; it is easier to tighten the hole afterwards if it has stretched out. Hem stitch around hole on the RS using split yarn. The bound-off sts will be invisible on both right and wrong sides.

Edgings and Bands with Facings

Always knit the first stitch except on the facings where you should slip the first st for a smooth edge that will be easier to sew up.

Usually the facing is knitted on smaller needles. Personally I prefer to have fewer sts for the facing. This is specified in the instructions when applicable.

When picking up across, pick up 1 st in each st across. When picking up downwards, 1 in each st/row would be too many. Usually I recommend: pick up 3 sts, skip 1, pick up 4 sts, skip 1. If there seem to be too many sts or more than calculated, you may need to pick up 3 sts more often than 4 sts, skipping 1 st between each group.

Don't forget that the single-color sections should be knitted more tightly than the patterned areas.

Finishing the Facings

Facings often have fewer sts than the body of a garment. When attaching the facing, the edging might bias or skew. Pin-baste and make sure that the edging is turned under neatly and that the sts on the outside match the corresponding sts on the inside all around or across.

Attach the facing behind the picked up sts, with 1 sewn stitch into each knit st. If the facing is too wide, the seam will pull in the knitting and be noticeable on the RS.

Small Split Necks

Machine-stitch down and back up again with 1 st between the seam lines (halfway in the next st); machine-stitch back a little to the side of the previous seam line (if these 2 seams are too close together, the sts might slide out). Cut open between the pairs of double lines.

Pick up and knit 3-4 sts and then skip 1 st. Always have 1 st at the base of the split neck.

Row 1: Knit (ridge).
Row 2: Knit, ssk over 2 sts before base st, knit base st, k2tog, finish row.
Row 3: Purl back.
Row 4: Purl (fold line), tightening yarn slightly when

working base st.
Row 5: Purl, pick up and knit 1 st at each side of the base st (make sure sts are not twisted).
Row 6: Knit, increasing 1 st on each side of base st.
Row 7: Purl.
If there is a color change and the second yarn hangs at the opposite side, be careful that knit and purl rows are correctly sequenced.

Bind off loosely around neck and slightly more loosely at base. Attach facing and seam bottom of split so that it lies flat.

Cutting "Steeks"

Sleeves: Use the same color as for the garment. Machine-stitch with small, tight sts, preferably a fine zigzag, and double seam with about 1/16 in / 1 mm distance between stitch lines. Stitch a little inside the edge of the cutting line. Cut between the seams.

Neckline: It is often tricky to keep the patterning consistent when working back and forth, as when shaping the neckline, for example. It is best to work the pattern all the way up. The neatest solution is to bind off the center stitch at the first decrease and work straight up from there. Use pins or a marking thread to indicate the neckline shaping. Check the pattern chart and machine-stitch 2 closely placed stitch lines. Make sure that the seam is inside the line where you will pick up and knit stitches for the neckband! Machine-stitch a slightly looser seam about 1/8 in / .25 cm inside the other lines. Cut open inside the inner stitch line.

Split Neck: Machine-stitch and cut as for sleeves, making sure that the stitching lines are reinforced at the base of the split.

Seams

Sew seams with split yarn. Using only some of the yarn plies makes a finer seam line and allows for tighter stitching without lumpiness. Sew 1 stitch into every knit stitch.

When attaching sleeves on right side of garment, use slightly finer yarn. You can split off a ply from the garment yarn.

Make sure that facings are folded straight across before sewing down so they don't bias. Pin facings down and then check both right and wrong sides to be sure that the stitches are aligned before sewing. If the facing is the same width as the garment edge, sew to the back of the edge, 1 stitch in each knit st. If the facing is wider than the edge, sew with a color to match the knitting. Carefully sew "stitch-wise" with split yarn.

Attaching Sleeves

Measure the width of sleeve top without stretching it. Measure down from shoulder for armhole depth. Machine-stitch twice down and up again around armhole and cut open between seam lines.

Make sure that the sleeve top fits comfortably at the shoulder so it doesn't pucker when the garment lies flat. I suggest that you lay the garment flat at the top of armhole, place a piece of cardboard between the layers, pin about 3 ¼-4 in / 8-10 cm, and then lay the whole armhole area flat and pin the rest of the sleeve in.

Usually sleeves are attached from the right side. There are always more rows on the body than on the sleeves.

If you have a garter edge: Sew 1 stitch into each knit stitch. If you are sewing inside or outside a garter ridge: Sew 1 stitch into each stitch inside the machine-stitched seam on the body.

The underarm can be a little tricky to sew into and it might be easier to knit the sections together instead. Seams are most often sewn inside or outside the lowest ridge of the sleeve facing, depending on whether or not the ridge should be visible. Sew the facing over the cut edge on WS, using split yarn.

Sleeve Length

If the sleeve cuffs are ribbed, it is usually not a problem if the sleeves are a little too long. However, if the sleeves have stockinette cuffs with a fold line, it is very important that the sleeves be exactly the right length. They can easily be too long and then a lovely pattern might be hidden under a crumpled turned-up cuff. You can usually determine how long the patterning on the sleeves will be. Try on the body of the sweater and calculate the sleeve length from that.

I-cords

You can knit a cord directly from the last 3 sts at the end of, for example, a cap.

CO 3 sts onto dpn. Always start from the same side of the needle. *Knit the sts, slide them back to front of needle, bring yarn around back and knit the sts; rep from *. Tighten the yarn slightly on the first st of each row so that the cord will be even.

End with k2tog, k1, slip 1st over 2nd; cut yarn and pull tight.

Striped I-cord

Make as for single-color cord, being careful to twist yarns around each other evenly when changing colors. Knit with one color, leave yarn at left, bring the other yarn under from the right side and knit the next row. Tighten the yarn slightly on the first st of each row.

Vertical Stripes with 1 or 2 Strands

Use an extra loose strand for each single stripe and knit it on every round up: With main color yarn to the left, bring the loose strand from the right and knit the st. Let this yarn hang to the left and bring the main color from the right and continue.

Sewn Loops

Thin loops placed closely together: First mark placement of loops. Hold the garment with RS facing and the edging up. Insert needle from below and up to beginning of loop's right side. Sew reinforcement stitches down and up so that the needle is centered on the edge. Sew a stitch to the left side and back to the right side. Sew a few reinforcement stitches from below and up so that the yarn is secured. Sew buttonhole stitch to the left, pushing the stitches together so that the loop is securely attached. It might bias after a while. Finally, insert the needle back and forth, pulling a little so that loop is even. Sew just one st through the loop and then insert needle a bit down on the back of the work and up again, so that it won't pull out with use. With needle in position for next loop, sew a little catching st down and up again and continue with the next loop.

Medium loops: Begin on the left side of the loop and lay down 3 strands to sew over. Catch yarn on every loop.

Thick loops: Beginning on right side, insert needle back and forth so that there are 4 strands to sew over.

If there is a large space between loops, secure yarn after each loop.

Knitted Buttons

Make a sample to determine sizing. Buttons begin with crochet and then are knitted tightly on fine needles.

Ch 5 and join into a ring with slip st. Ch 1 and sc 11 into ring. Push sts together so they will all fit. Join with slip st.

Working into back loop of each sc, pick up 11 sts + the last st on crochet hook onto dpn = 4 sts on each needle. Join and knit 2 rnds. On the next rnd, k1f&b into each st = 24 sts. For a rounded edge, knit 1 more rnd and then cut yarn. Beginning with another needle (to avoid holes), change colors, knit 1 rnd, and then purl 1 rnd on RS. For a smoother look, knit back, wrap yarn around next st and turn. Knit 2 more rnds. On the next rnd, *k2tog, k1*; rep from * to * around = 16 sts. Knit 2 rnds, cut yarn and pull through rem sts.

Single-color buttons: Knit 4 rnds, decrease and continue as above.

Twist and secure the 2 strands outside the little hole. The yarn tail in the center can be used to attach the button. Insert a plastic ring into the button; tighten and secure yarn tail. Sew securely between the layers with the center yarn tail. The ring should be the same color as the yarn or slightly darker. It is possible to dye plastic rings with waterproof India ink or you can use a flat button (with or without a shank) instead of the plastic ring—try it!

Pompoms

Wrap the yarn about 30 times around 3 fingers held together, cut yarn (otherwise it will be too thick). Use split yarn to tie around the wrapped yarn, sewing it securely back and forth through all the strands so they are held tightly together. Secure with sewing thread and begin cutting from the inside out, and then shake pompom to round it out.

When attaching a pompom, the yarns should be secured so that they won't slip out. Spread the yarns and sew up and down in several places on the pompom so that it won't shift out of place. Finally, hold the pompom yarns out of the way and attach the cord to the pompom, sewing back and forth to secure cord.

Level of Difficulty

Each design has a number indicating the level of difficulty: 1 is the easiest and 5 the hardest.

Charts

Charts are read from the bottom row and up, beginning at the lower right hand corner. Arrows indicate

beginning and ending points for patterns as necessary for different sizes. Many of the charts in this book show several color options. Use the same main and contrast colors you have chosen across/around the entire piece. All of the patterns here are two-color stranded knitting, not intarsia, unless specifically indicated. There are, however, some patterns that have 3 colors within a row.

Abbreviations

BO	bind off	MC	main color
CC	contrast color	mm	millimeter(s)
ch	chain, chain st (crochet)	ndl(s)	needle(s)
		p	purl
cm	centimeter(s)	pm	place marker
CO	cast on	rem	remain(ing)
dec	decrease	rep	repeat
dpn	double-pointed needle(s)	rnd(s)	round(s)
		RS	right side
in	inch(es)	sc	single crochet
inc	increase	sskslip,	slip, knit: (slip 1 st
k	knit		knitwise) 2 times,
k1f&b	knit into front and then back of stitch		slide sts to left needle and knit
k2tog	knit 2 together		into back loops
k2tog tbl	knit 2 together through back loops or work ssk instead	st(s)	stitch(es)
		tbl	through back loop(s)
m1	make 1: lift strand between two stitches and knit into back loop	WS	wrong side

Correcting small problems and mistakes

—and how to avoid making the worst of them…

Perhaps it is unnerving to be presented with all one's bad habits in their own section—and then to have someone call them "problems!" Of course you are free to do as you've always done but many will certainly agree with me that some of the following are "mistakes." Just remember that yarn is expensive and it takes a lot of hours to knit it up. For that reason, it is well worth taking a little extra time to create garments you'll be proud of.

Poor quality circular needles
If there is a gap between the metal and plastic, the yarn will catch there and some of the fibers will shed out. This results in a hairy-looking garment especially if you knit rather tightly. Find out which side of the circular is best and hold it in your left hand.

Cast-on is too tight
The first cast-on method I learned was the knit cast-on. Later I learned how to cast on with two strands of yarn (long-tail) which seemed more "grown-up." Often, however, the long-tail cast-on is too tight which is particularly problematic at the lower edge of a sweater. It could be so tight that you can't get the sweater on or the sweater droops like a bag over the cast-on edge. Uneven tension in the cast-on also shows all too clearly. The strands extend over 2 stitches and so it is impossible to pick up stitches directly from the cast-on row. If you use the technique learned in childhood (knit cast-on), the cast-on edge will always be smooth and elastic.

Binding off is too tight
The usual method for binding off can easily be too tight. On short stretches (for example, buttonholes, base of split neck, pockets, etc.), the regular method works just fine. Using the same bind-off on sleeve caps, necklines, etc, can be catastrophic. There is nothing worse than trying to fit your head through a tight neckline.

Knitting too loosely
Knitting gauge is very important and must be consistent. Single-color knitting should be worked slightly more tightly than pattern knitting, but not the opposite! Wavy lower edges or a billowing front can ruin an otherwise well-knit garment.

Knitting too tightly
One common mistake is knitting pattern motifs too tightly. If the strands are caught often, the garment will be more elastic. Do not stack caught strands above one another—that looks messy and small dots of color will appear on the right side.

Loose "ridges"
On many garments, garter stitch ridges are decorative elements or hide the line around the neck where stitches were picked up with a contrasting color. Make sure that the ridges are actually decorative and not just loose, wavy stripes. To avoid this problem, work a little more tightly on the WS rows.

Stranding across too many stitches
Who hasn't pulled on a sweater only to catch a button with the yarn floats…
For children's garments, it is best to catch floats every 3 or maybe 4 stitches. Do not twist the yarns around each other at the same place on every row—it will definitely show on the right side.

If the garment has a facing, then you can strand over 5 stitches (but no more) because the floats will be covered by the facing.

Knots
Do not secure yarn tails by knotting them together. The knots can loosen or show as a thick spot, even under a facing.

When millspun yarn has knots, it is tempting to leave the knots on the wrong side. However, it is better to cut the yarn and splice in a new strand. When these small tails are spit-spliced, they can then be caught as for stranded floats. There are a couple of ways to splice yarn neatly:
1. Leaving a tail of about 4-6 in / 10-15 cm on old and new strands, take new strand and begin knitting. After a few rows, weave in the tails on WS. Weave tail through 5-6 sts; turn, weave back; turn and weave a third time. This locks the tail in. Be careful that the weaving does not show on RS.

2. To spit splice: unravel 2-3 in / 5-7.5 cm from the end of each yarn, pull out a ply or two from each yarn and feather the ends. Overlap the ends, interlocking ends from each yarn. Spit (delicately, of course) onto the overlap area and then briskly rub the yarn between your hands until the yarn ends felt together. Roll in the direction of the twist to firm up the yarn.

Securing yarn ends
Do not trim yarn ends too short. The yarn can slide out again and then there will be a hole. If necessary sew back over the end to secure it. Make sure it is not too thick and doesn't show on the right side.

Long stitches
When a facing is sewn down, it should be is as elastic as the rest of the garment. If the stitches are too long, the seam line can pull in as for a tight cast-on. Seam with short, but not too tight, stitches.

Thick seams
Split the yarn. Most of the yarns used for the garments in this book are 4-ply (Peer Gynt is 5-ply). When attaching sleeves, remove one ply of the yarn or use half the strand. This will bring the stitches closer together.

Patterns don't match at the sides
The yarn is twisted and the piece biases as you knit. It is not good enough to lay the garment flat, machine-stitch, and cut. Make sure that the side stitches match precisely.

The pattern is not placed the same way on each sleeve
This is the same problem with biasing described above. Find the center st on each sleeve and make sure that it is attached at the shoulder seam.

The sleeve cap is attached too tightly
If you lay the sleeve and body flat, the sleeve seam can end up too tight at the cap and the shoulder seam stands out in a little point. First lay the top part of the shoulder and sleeve flat, pin out about 3 ¼-4 in / 8-10 cm. Then lay the rest of the armhole area flat and pin out.

Loose shoulders
Many patterns suggest Kitchener stitch for joining shoulder seams. This makes a smooth finishing but, if you join too loosely, the shoulder seams will droop over the shoulders. An extra edging at the top allows for a more durable seam. You can then finish with either Kitchener st or three-needle bind-off.

You should be aware that, with a Kitchener st seam, the stitches are offset by one half stitch and patterns will not meet exactly. On the other hand, with three-needle bind-off (if you follow the instructions) the patterns will always meet precisely.

Buttonholes are too tight
Bind off loosely for buttonholes (see section about buttonholes on page 2). Do not use buttonhole stitch around the holes as it can be too tight. Use hem stitch on the right side, making sure that the bound-off sts are covered.

Polar Light

Women's
Long Jacket/Coat
Cap

Level of Difficulty: 3-4

Sizes	S	(M)	L	(XL)
Chest	47 ¼ in/120 cm	(52 in/132 cm)	54 ¼ in/138 cm	(56 in/142 cm)
Length	30 ¾ in/78 cm	(31 in/79 cm)	31 ½ in/80 cm	(32 in/81 cm)
Sleeve length	18 ½ in/47 cm	(19 in/48 cm)	19 in/48 cm	(19 ¼ in/49 cm)

Note: Work total length to measurements listed above or desired length. Try on garment and adjust sleeve length as necessary.

Yarn: Peer Gynt (100% wool, 98 yds / 91 m per 50 g), 2 colors. The model shown is worked with black 1099 (CC) and dark rust 4049 (MC). Work as charted or reverse colors.

Yarn amounts

Jacket/Coat:	S	(M)	L	(XL)
MC:	17 balls	18 balls	19 balls	21 balls
CC:	12 balls	13 balls	14 balls	16 balls

Cap: 2 balls MC and 1-2 balls CC

Needles: US size 4 / 3.5 mm – 32 in / 80 cm circular for body and shorter circular + set of dpn for sleeves. Short circular or dpn US sizes 2 and 4 / 3 and 3.5 mm for cap.

Gauge: 22 sts and approx 27 rows = 4 x 4 in / 10 x 10 cm. Adjust needle size to obtain correct gauge.

Notions: 6 pewter buttons "Hardanger;" heavy snap.

LONG JACKET/COAT
Body
Charts A, B, and C.
Diagonal lines on the chart = CC
With MC and long circular, cast on 296 (318) 329 (340) sts. Join, being careful not to twist cast-on row. Knit 10 rnds in stockinette. Note: The last 4 sts of the round are the "steek" and are worked as: k1, p2, k1 throughout. These sts will be cut later for center front opening.

On the next rnd, increase (with m1 after approximately every 11th st—do not increase over steek sts): 27 (29) 30 (31) sts evenly spaced around = 323 (347) 359 (371) sts. Knit 1 round and then purl 1 rnd for fold line.
Now work following chart A:
Note: The front is worked the same way for all sizes. In order to center the pattern on the back, begin the other sections of the pattern as

indicated on the chart for the various sizes.
Work the right front first = 49 sts. Next work the sides/back: 221 (245) 257 (269) sts, beginning at arrow for desired size. The panel should be the same at each side. I have also marked the finishing point for each size.
End round with the 49 sts for left front, working to mirror image right front + the 4 steek sts.

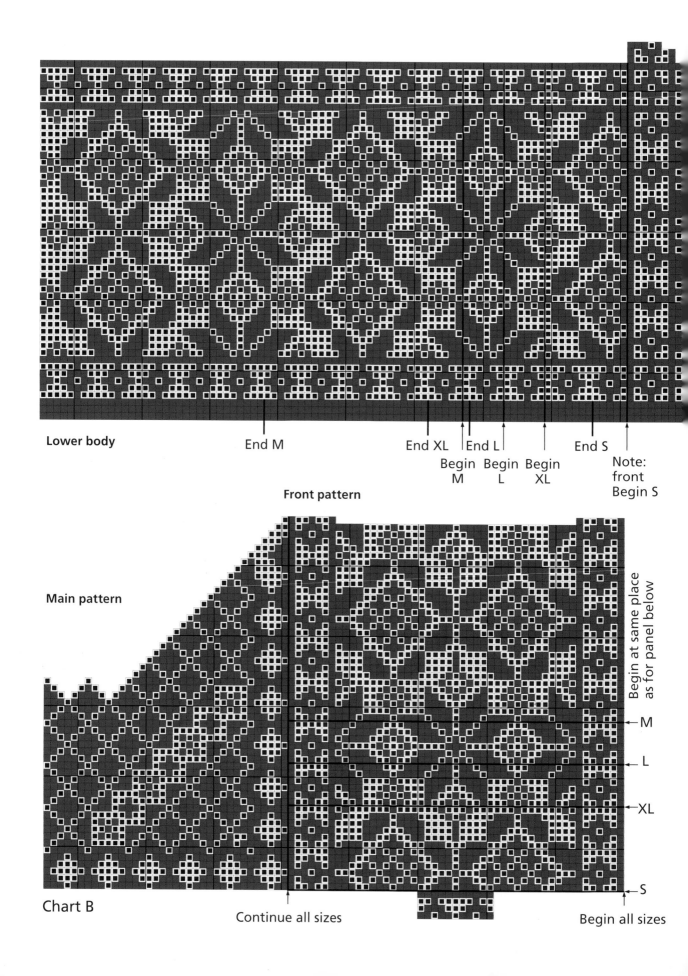

Lower body

End M

End XL | End L

Begin M | Begin L | Begin XL

End S

Note: front Begin S

Front pattern

Main pattern

Begin at same place as for panel below

← M

← L

← XL

← S

Chart B

Continue all sizes

Begin all sizes

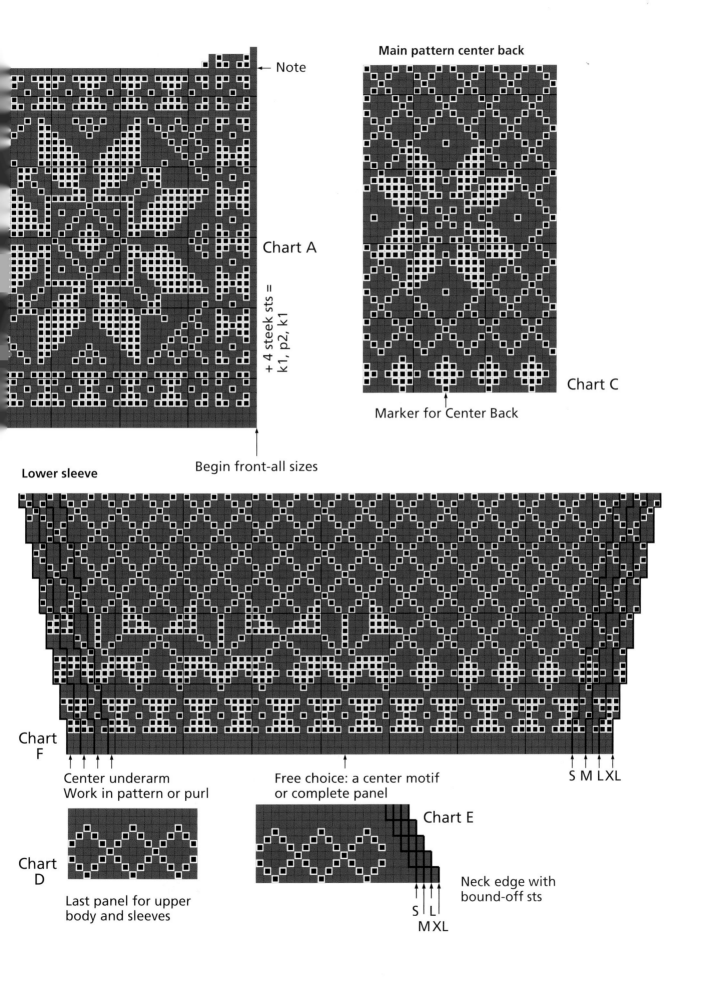

Note

Main pattern center back

Chart A

+ 4 steek sts =
k1, p2, k1

Chart C

Marker for Center Back

Begin front-all sizes

Lower sleeve

Chart
F

Center underarm
Work in pattern or purl

Free choice: a center motif
or complete panel

S M L XL

Chart E

Chart
D

Last panel for upper
body and sleeves

Neck edge with
bound-off sts

S   L
M XL

Work to the point marked "Note" on top chart of chart A.

Now work charts B and C. Place a marker at each side of st 85 (91) 94 (105).

Count out from both sides to place pattern motifs correctly. "Rose" patterns are worked up each front while the sides and back are a diagonal block pattern; the stitches of chart C are centered on back. Also mark the center back st. Make sure that the sts match at the rose pattern. The first rnd after "note" has already been knitted.

The front pattern begins at exactly the same place as the side pattern below. Begin at the arrow for your size and work the 49 sts of front. Continue the rest of the pattern (to the left for the front pattern on the chart, with diagonal lines) at the same place for all sizes. The pattern work can be somewhat difficult at the beginning but do not lose heart. Work for 2 in / 5 cm and then, on the back only, dec at each side. Work the first dec (after right side st) as ssk, and the other (before left side st), k2tog. Work decreases every 2 in / 5 cm a total of 6 times at each side = 12 sts deceased on back. Move the markers at sides up every 2 in / 5 cm. After completing decreases, the patterns will match again.

Continue without further shaping to the neck edge at the front. Bind off the 4 steek sts and place the 49 sts of each front onto a holder. Count 49 sts towards center back and pm at each side of these. Find the center st between these marked sts and the front opening. These side sts should be at the center of a block. BO these sts at each side. The pattern and number of sts should match for front and back shoulders. From this point on, work back and forth, working the back and each front separately. Cast on 1 extra (edg) st at neck opening. Work 18-20 rows in pattern on each section.

Finish the fronts as shown on chart D. Purl 1 row on RS and then work in stockinette with MC for 2 in / 5 cm for facing. BO loosely. The back should round a little at the neck. Finish the pattern and then work 1 row with a single color. On the next row, BO the center 43 sts. Work to bound-off sts; turn, BO 3 sts, purl back on RS.

The shoulder facing will now extend across the entire back.

Work 2 rows and then increase 3 sts towards neck opening. Repeat on the other side, casting on 38 sts between the two pieces. Work for another 1 ¼ in / 3 cm and then BO loosely.

Finishing

Machine-stitch and cut open at center front. Work both front facing bands the same way. Sew facing down at lower edge, using split yarn. With MC, pick up and knit sts down the front, going into both layers at the facing. Pick up 4 sts for every 5 rows. Knit back. The edge should not be wavy or pull in. If either is the case, rip out and try again. Work in stockinette to the same width as front edging panel and then BO loosely.

Turn facings under and sew down. Join shoulders with three-needle bind-off. Sew down shoulder facing.

Neckband

Chart E shows the continuation of the front pattern.

The front pattern should continue directly into the neck but the back has a panel matching the main pattern. On the 3 final rows of the band, there is patterning on the front but the back is single color. If necessary, mark the sides.

Place the 49 front sts on a needle. At side of neck, pick up and knit 15-16 sts, pick up and knit 51 sts along the back, 15-16 sts on side of neck, and then work the 49 sts of other

front. Pick up through both layers if there is a facing. There should now be a total of 179-181 sts.

Note: The panel should look as if it continues directly from the back pattern and it is important to pick up and knit sts in the center of a st. Count out from center st of the back so that you know where the neckband panel should begin. The first block should be complete (see chart E). Four different places are marked for the beginning point. Make sure there are the same number of sts on each side and begin at the arrow corresponding to that number of sts.

Work the first 49 sts in front pat-

Cap, Pattern and Shaping

Chart G

← Fold line

8 repeats = 112 sts

tern. Ssk the last st with the next. Work the necessary number of sts and then neckband E. Check once more to be sure the patterns match on the back!

The pattern reverses on the other side—k2tog to match previous ssk then work remaining 48 sts of front pattern.

On every RS row, dec "diagonally" towards the front neck until 1 block has been completed. Purl back but continue only the front pattern; the rest is worked in a single color. Add an extra CC strand on the other side for the 3 last rows.

Fold line: knit 1 row and then purl 1 row on RS. Work facing in one color, increasing to match previous decreases. BO loosely purlwise on RS.

Sleeves

Charts F and D.

With MC and short circular or dpn, CO 66 (70) 74 (78) sts. Join, being careful not to twist cast-on row. Work 18 rnds for facing, decreasing 2 sts at underarm (on each side of 2 underarm sts) on rnds 5, 10, and 15 = 60 (64) 68 (72) sts rem. On the next rnd, increase 8 sts evenly spaced around to 68 (72) 76 (80) sts. Knit 1 rnd and then work picot fold line: *k2tog, yo*; rep * to * around. Now work following chart F. You can choose the patterning here. You can work the star panel all around, or 1 star at the center, or the stars can be eliminated. Choose the pattern you like and continue, increasing 1 st at each side of 2 center underarm sts on every 5th rnd 7 times, every 4th rnd 7 times, and then every 3rd rnd until there are 124 (128) 132 (136) sts. Work new sts into pattern. Try on the sleeve with it pinned to jacket body. Continue until sleeve is desired length and finish as shown on chart D. Purl 5 rnds on RS for facing. Bind off sleeve as explained in Techniques. Sew down facing. Make other sleeve the same way.

Finishing

Measure top of sleeve; half the width = armhole depth. Measure depth of armhole down from shoulder seam and then machine-stitch and cut armholes. Attach sleeves from RS. Sew down facings on WS, covering cut edges of armhole with sleeve cap facing.

Make button loops at front and sew on buttons. Sew on a heavy snap at the top of the innermost layer near the neckband. If you want the flap to fold out, the snap can be sewn a little further down.

CAP

With MC and smaller dpn, CO 102 sts; join and then knit 11 rnds. On the next rnd, increase after every 10th st to 112 sts. Knit 1 rnd and then make 1 ridge (= purl 1 rnd on RS) with CC. Change to larger needles and continue in cap border panel, chart G = 8 repeats of 14 st repeat). After completing chart G, knit 1 rnd in MC.

On the next rnd, begin crown shaping. On the first increase rnd, inc by k1f&b (so that the stripe pattern isn't distorted). On the second inc rnd, inc with m1. Inc and dec on each side of the "post" as shown on the chart. When 32 sts rem, k2tog around. Knit 2 rnds and then k2tog around. Make a short I-cord with the rem 8 sts. Cut yarn and pull through rem sts. Fold facing at ridge and sew down smoothly on WS. It is okay if the edge aligns with the last rnd of pattern color.

Selbu Knitting

IN THE OLD DAYS

In about 1850, the "mother" of Selbu knitting, Marit Emstad, knitted her first pair of two-color patterned mittens. She was only 11 years old but was clever enough to master this previously unknown technique. She began with a very simple design, probably inspired by embroidery or weaving. After the technique became more well-known in her town, more and more knitted with two colors and a number of patterns developed, inspired by the landscape and the knitter's surroundings. These patterns were named after the source of the inspiration or for the person who had developed them. Popular sources of inspiration were the gold colored decorations on sewing machines, milk separators, etc., leading to, for example, "separator hook" pattern. Natural objects also inspired patterns such as "snow crystal," flower blossom" and "spruce branch."

If a pattern was repeated over a large area, it was called an "endless rose." "Tyrrillen," the end of the rod on a butter churn was a good source of inspiration for rose patterns and there are countless variants of "Chantilly rose." The best known pattern is the eight-petal rose or "Radiant Rose" popularly called a "Selbu rose." It is an ancient symbol for the star of Bethlehem and is recognizable in many techniques the world over.

The first mittens would have been knitted with handspun yarn in natural white and sheep's black. The yarn was finely spun and the needles were quite a bit finer than those we use today.

With so many stitches on each needle, the pattern could be much more detailed and varied than now. Eventually, stockings were also knit but seldom with the same patterns as for the mittens. Sweaters and jackets were not produced until the inter-war period. They were fashioned after Fana and Setesdal sweaters but embellished with Selbu's own pattern traditions.

After a while millspun yarn was used instead of the fine handspun and the patterns were simplified. Fortunately, not all of these mittens and socks and caps were worn out and many of the oldest garments are preserved. They continue to be admired and enjoyed, an inspiration for our own and future generations.

The simplest of the preserved garments have red and black yarn. They were actually knitted in black and white and then dyed afterwards. However, dye was expensive if it had to be bought and many didn't want to spend time hunting for dye plants when dyeing wasn't necessary. These dyed mittens were undoubtedly made for wedding gifts and special occasions.

BRIDAL CUSTOMS IN SELBU

A prospective bride in Selbu had to prepare her wedding in good time. The bridegroom and his whole family should each receive a pair of long stockings and everyone who helped during the wedding would be given a pair of mittens. The bride had to knit these herself and hastily done work was shameful.

A few days before the wedding fest all the women invited came with a pair of knitted mittens. The bride hung these up by a cord in the "bridal loft," so that all the guests could see and admire them during the party which lasted 2-3 days. When it was time for the guests to go home, the bride gave out the mittens. Each man had to get the mittens his wife made and it was no easy task to remember which mittens belonged to whom. The young girls divided their mittens among the young men. It was not uncommon to display 80-100 pairs of mittens and perhaps 15-20 pairs of stockings. If the bride made a mistake when giving out the garments, she was thought to have behaved stupidly!

This custom offers the most likely explanation for the tradition of knitting particularly fine mittens and stockings in Selbu. The small garments to go on display for the wedding were made with extra skill and care because it was important to make a good impression. Young women had a special reason to show how accomplished they were with their very fine mittens or stockings.

Coffee Bean

Women's Jacket with hood/ cap
Poncho with hood/cap
Mittens
Leg Warmers

Level of Difficulty: Knitting 2-3; finishing 5

Sizes	XS-S	(S-M)	M-L
Chest	45 in/114 cm	(47 ¾ in/121 cm)	50 ¾ in/129 cm
Length	21 ¼ (22) in/54 (56) cm	22 ¾ (23 ¾) in/58 (60) cm	24 ½ (25 ¼ in/62 (64) cm
Sleeve length	15 ¾ in/40 cm	(16 ½ in/42 cm)	17 in/43 cm

Yarn: Peer Gynt (100% wool, 98 yds / 91 m per 50 g): Black 1099, red 4228
Hood lining: Telemark (100% wool, 153 yds / 140 m per 50 g (note: Telemark is no longer available) 4328

Yarn Amounts
Jacket *(amounts are given for short version; for a longer jacket, purchase 1-2 balls extra of each color)*

	XS-S	(S-M)	M-L
MC	13 balls	14 balls	15 balls
CC	4 balls	5 balls	5 balls

Poncho (one size): 22 balls MC and 1-2 balls CC
Hood/Cap (one size): 3 balls MC, 2 balls CC, 2 balls Telemark
Mittens (one size): 1 ball each MC and CC
Leg Warmers (one size): 2 balls each MC and CC

Needles: US size 4 / 3.5 mm – long and short circulars + dpn; US 2 / 3 mm for hood lining (circular and dpn). Crochet hook and/or circular 1 size smaller (US 3 / 3.25 mm) for picking up sts.

Gauge: Normally this yarn is knitted at 22 sts per 4 in / 10 cm but it should be knitted more tightly for this garment. The number of sts is calculated at about 23-24 sts per 4 in / 10 cm or 24 sts to 4 in / 10 cm for a single color. The poncho is knitted more loosely. Adjust needle size to obtain correct gauge.

Notions: 24-25 pewter buttons, "Sissel," small, for jacket/hood. 7 extra buttons for the poncho. Knitted cords.

JACKET WITH HOOD/CAP
This model is made with specially knitted button loops at the front. Try a sample to see if you can make them satisfactorily. Of course you could make the more usual sewn heavy loops instead, as for the hood/cap and poncho.
The jacket can be made as long as desired (the shortest version is shown). If you want it longer, work 1 or 2 extra repeats (1-2 red and 1-2 black stripes).

Body

With black, CO 216 (230) 243 sts; join, being careful not to twist cast-on row. Work in stockinette for 2 ¾ in / 7 cm for facing. At the same time, after 1 ¼–1 ½ in / 3–3.5 cm make a buttonhole. Work 15 sts, BO 3, continue across. On the next row, cast on 3 new sts over the bound-off sts. On the next-to-last row, increase 15 (16) 17 sts evenly spaced around (inc after about every 14th st) for a total of 231 (246) 260 sts. Make fold line by purling on RS. Work the edging with black in stockinette for 2 ¾ in / 7 cm and don't forget the buttonhole spaced as for facing.

After completing facing and edging, increase 62 (65) 69 sts to 293 (311) 329 sts.

Note: If you inc after every 4th st, you'll be short by 4 sts; simply inc these 4 sts on the next row. Knit 2 rnds and begin pattern A at the arrow and finish at the same place on the other side of the steek. The last 4 sts of the rnd are the steek and are knitted with both colors of yarn held together on pattern rounds. Do not work pattern motifs over the 4 steek sts. The pattern is a multiple of 9+2 (first 2 black squares on chart) + 8 stitches (to balance pattern on other side of front). After the first 2 sts on chart, (work sts 3–11) 31 (33) 35 times and end rnd with with the first motif + 2 sts MC + the 4 steek sts. Work 7 (9) 11 stripes in pattern (rows 1–18 of chart A), beginning and ending with a black background stripe. After completing stripes, work in lice pattern (top 6 rows of chart A) up to underarm, about 12 ¼ (12 ¾) 13 in / 31 (32) 33 cm or 14 ½ (15) 15 ½ in / 37 (38) 39 cm from lower edge.

Underarm shaping: Work 72 (75) 78 sts, BO 10 (13) 16 sts for underarm, work 125 (131) 137 sts, BO 10 (13) 16 sts for other underarm, work 72 (75) 78 sts (numbers include st

left each after bind-off) and then BO the 2 center steek sts. Now work back and forth in lice pattern, working each front and the back separately. To keep the lice pattern even, knit the outermost st at each edge with both yarns (these sts will be hidden later).

At the same time, shape armhole by binding off at side: 2-2-1-1 (3-2-1-1) 3-2-2-1 sts = 66 (68) 70 sts + steek rem for one front. Continue on the front until you've worked a total of 42 rows from beginning of armhole. Next, shape neckline.

Neck shaping: At neck edge, BO 23-3-2-1-1 sts (the first st is a steek st that hadn't been eliminated previously). There should now be 37 (39) 41 sts on front.

Note: Finish the lice patterning just before the last decrease row for sizes S and M. Size L: work 1 more lice row.

The shoulder pattern will be worked here later. The shoulder section is worked in pattern from the back. The front is worked in a single color for the rest of the shoulder plus the facing which extends under the patterning on the back.

Work another 10 (12) 14 rows with MC without lice. Work other front to correspond.

CO 3 new sts at neck edge and then CO 30 sts between the two parts of the front (back facing for the back neck/back). Work 7 rows in stockinette and then BO loosely.

Back

Shape armholes as for front and work a total of about 47 (49) 51 rows from beginning of underarm; finish with 2 rows black.

Knit 1 ridge with red and then 2 rows black in stockinette.

Work chart B: The outermost st at each side is worked with both yarns. At back neck, BO as shown on chart (first BO 33 sts at center back and then 3 sts at each side of back neck). Continue, working each

side separately. Work 2 rows stockinette with black and then 1 ridge (knit 2 rows) with red. BO with black. This will later be joined at the front. Don't weave in the yarn tails around the armhole yet. Work other back shoulder to correspond.

Sleeves

The increases at the top of the sleeves are worked in black, so it is difficult to see where the shaping is. On the model we've used a combination of increase methods. Knit into front and back (k1f&b) of a stitch to increase unless it is a lice st; in that case, increase with m1.

With black and short circular or dpn, CO 51 (53) 55 sts; join, being careful not to twist cast-on row. Knit 1 rnd and change to red. Work (2 rnds red, 2 rnds black) 3 times. On the next rnd (with black), increase evenly spaced around to 57 (59) 61 sts. Change to red and work 1 rnd as follows for picot fold line: K1, *yo, k2tog*; rep * to * around. Change back to black and knit 2 rnds followed by cuff pattern on chart C. Purl 1 rnd with red for a ridge (last rnd on chart) and then continue with black.

On the next rnd, inc 10 (14) 18 sts.

Inc more closely together at the outside of the sleeve than on the inside. Find the center st of the sleeve – this should be a lice st. Now count out from it to the underarm. Begin working lice on every 3rd rnd. At the same time, increase at underarm at each side of the 2 center underarm sts on every 3rd rnd 6 (4) 2 times and then on every 4th rnd until there are a total of 113 (119) 125 sts. Now work back and forth. BO 8 (14) 20 sts centered at underarm. Dec at each side: 3 sts 4 times, 4 sts 3 times, and 5 sts 3 times (78 sts decreased). BO rem 27 sts; do not weave in tails yet. Work the other sleeve the same way and set sleeves aside.

Finishing

Body: Lay the uppermost part flat. Attach the panel at the front (from the back) overlapping about 2 rows over the top lice row, and sew from RS (as invisibly as possible). Use Kitchener stitch for the smoothest join. Remove 1 strand (of the yarn's 5 plies) so that it will be a bit thinner. Pin-baste (preferably with T-pins), making sure the patterns match. Stitch back so that the bound-off edge is hidden.
Note: When Kitchener weaving two pieces of knitting, stitches are offset

by ½ stitch. Make sure that this shift is mirror image (it may not be obvious at first). Sew down shoulder facing on WS so that it covers the red ridge on the back. Don't forget that all the facings are tighter, especially over the shoulders, so the pattern knitting should have more ease than the facings. Otherwise, the ridges and pattern panels will look tight and "stretched."

Machine-stitch and cut front. Sew down facing at lower edge with split yarn. With black, pick up and knit sts down or up front edge, picking up 4 sts for every 5 rows. Pick up sts through both layers at facings. Knit back (1 ridge) and then work in stockinette for 6 rows. Bind off the bottom st (over lower facing), continue to a total of 26 rows, BO. Work other side the same way. Steam press jacket front where the facing will be. This side is wide, so you should pin baste it at the fold line before sewing it down or it might bias.

Neckband

Note: Make sure that your gauge is correct. It is important that the single color neckband is worked at 24 sts to 4 in / 10 cm.
With red, pick up and knit sts. Pick up 1 st in each st at front and back; at the sides skip every 5th st for a total of 133 (137) 141 sts. Make sure there are the same number of sts on each side of neck opening. The sts sometimes "twist" differently. Over the doubled knitting, pick up through both layers and check the back to make sure the stitches are picked up correctly. It is a good idea to use T-pins all the way around the back so that is doesn't shift. Hold the crochet hook as perpendicular as possible over the knitting. If it is too angled, it can shift the sts incorrectly. The jacket overlaps by about 21 sts on each side of front. With red, knit

back = 1 ridge, making sure the ridge isn't too loose and then work 5 rows stockinette with black. Make 1 buttonhole on the right side, positioning it over previous buttonhole (see section on buttonholes in Techniques). The buttonhole is worked over 3 sts, 15 sts inside the edge: work until 18 sts rem, BO 3, complete row. Next row: K15, CO 3, complete row. Work 5 more rows, leave the black yarn hanging, and make 1 ridge with red (fold line). Work facing to same width as band. On the 3rd row, dec 1 st at each shoulder and at center back (the facing should be a bit narrower than the edge). Don't forget to make a buttonhole on 6th row of facing. Bind off loosely. Sew down facing and sew around the buttonhole with split yarn.

Joining sleeves and body

With RS facing and black, pick up sts around sleeve cap using a needle one size smaller than for garment knitting. Pick up a total of 135 (141) 147 sts. It may be a little tight in the bound-off or turned sts. If the bound-off sts are red, try to pick them up so they look like a knit stitch and not a crooked dot. Some of the sts might look a bit loose but will tighten up when you knit back. Working rather tightly, knit back with black = 1 ridge; leave yarn hanging and set sleeve aside. Do the same with the other sleeve.

The next step will seem a bit complicated but it is worth trying. If it is impossible to get the right number of sts around the sleeves, you can sew them in as usual (see explanation below), but first try the following:
Make sure you have good lighting and bite your tongue…
With red, pick up sts around the armhole, using a smaller needle than for body. You must pick up exactly the same number of sts as

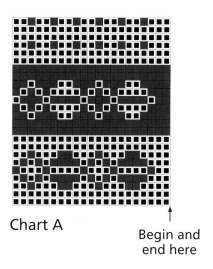

Chart A

Begin and end here

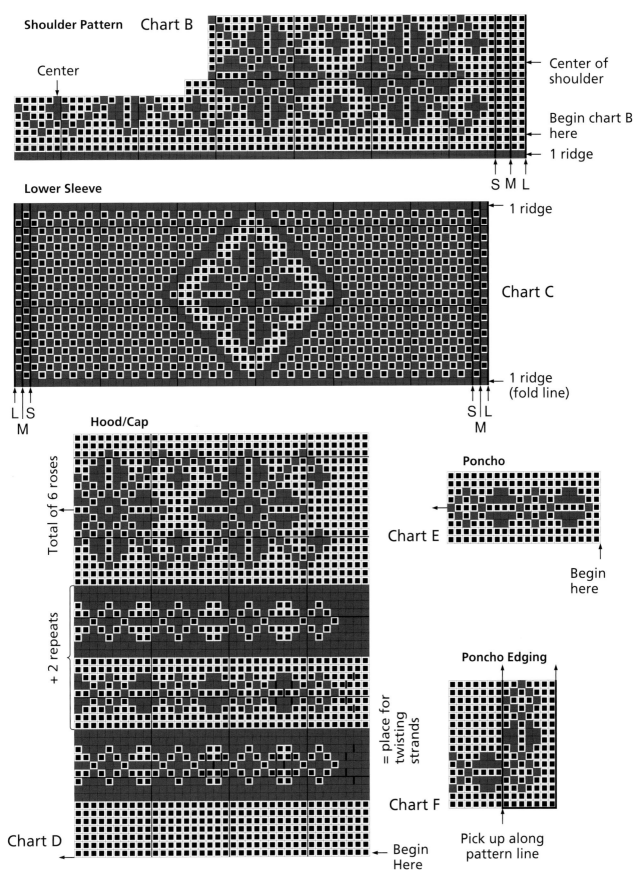

Shoulder Pattern Chart B

Center

Center of shoulder

Begin chart B here

1 ridge

S M L

Lower Sleeve

1 ridge

Chart C

1 ridge (fold line)

L S
M

S L
M

Hood/Cap

Total of 6 roses

+ 2 repeats

= place for twisting strands

Chart D

Begin Here

Poncho

Chart E

Begin here

Poncho Edging

Chart F

Pick up along pattern line

19

for sleeves = 135 (141) 147 sts. Beginning at center of underarm, pick up in each bound-off st. Continue around, picking up 4 sts and skipping 1. When about 3 ½-4 in / 9-10 cm from the shoulder facing and again about 3 ½-4 / 9-10 cm past it, pick up through every st. Don't forget to hold the crochet hook perpendicular when inserting it through two layers of knitting, or it will shift. It is also important not to work too loosely or pull in the sts, especially at the top. Continue to the other side the same way. Write down the stitch counts as you move them onto the needles so you don't lose track. Check the number of sts on each side, and make sure you have the same number for the other sleeve. There will be a few more sts on the front than on the back.

If there are too few sts around, you have to rip out the row to the point where you picked up sts in each st and start over. I had to do this three times before it worked out but it was certainly worth the extra trouble for a smoother seam and it was in fact easier!

When the st count is correct, sew/knit across so that there are exactly the same number of sts on each side. Count from the red ridge and down.

Knit back rather tightly = 1 red ridge; cut yarn.

The sleeve and body can now be joined. Turn the body so that it and the sleeve are RS facing RS and the body is towards you. Use the black yarn from the sleeve and join with three-needle bind-off (see Techniques). It is not necessary to join the facings. Weave in all yarn ends.

Loops

You can make either sewn or knitted loops. The last is the most difficult. Begin the first loop immediately beyond the buttonhole on lower edge. The next loop should be at the lowest black stripe, and then at

Tab, Poncho

Chart G

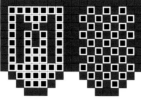 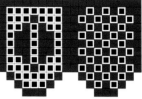

Initial   "Coffee Bean"

each black strip above. Space the rest above so that there is 1 loop on the neckband and 1 below this. The 2 topmost and the 2 lowest loops should be closer together than the others. Be especially careful with the top loops and reinforce them. There will be loops around the hood and neck, see Finishing for Hood/Cap.

Sewn loops: see Techniques.

Knitted button loops

The topmost loop (on the neckband) should not be knitted; it must be sewn. A knitted loop here takes up too much space for the hood. Space the loops as specified above. Where there are stripes, there should be 6 "bumps" between each loop. It doesn't matter if there are 5, 7, or 8 bumps between the lice. The most important consideration is that the topmost loops under the neckband are alike. Leave about 8 in / 20 cm yarn tail (to be used later for securing the loops).

With crochet hook and black yarn, pick up 9 sts along the outermost "bumps" of the fold line, CO 9 sts beside them, divide sts onto 4 smaller size dpn. Knit 1 round. On the next rnd, BO the 3 center sts, at both front and back of the loop. Make sure that the loop looks neat and smooth (see section on buttonholes in Techniques). Make 3 half hitches over the holes instead

of casting on 3 new sts. Knit 2 ½ rnds, shaping top as for a mitten. The shaping begins at the back. BO until 6 sts remain, cut yarn and pull through rem sts. Weave in ends at tip or they will be in the way.

Sew down tab from the inside. Split the yarn and use one half for sewing and the other for stitching a little back and forth inside the edge to secure it well. On the other side, where the yarn tail was left hanging, pull in a bit.

Finish by sewing around each buttonhole.

Sew on all the buttons on the jacket (except for around neck).

HOOD/CAP

Work in the same gauge as for jacket. The side of the hood will be lined so it isn't necessary to twist the yarns; floats over 4 sts are fine. With black, CO 110 sts; join, being careful not to twist cast-on row. Knit 8 rnds for facing and then purl 1 rnd on RS for fold line. Knit 4 rnds. On the next rnd, increase on every 10th st to 121 sts. Knit 2 rnds and then change to red.

Now work following Chart D. The last 2 sts of the round are the steek and should always be knitted with both yarns. Begin and end at the arrow. There should be a total of 7 stripes with the main color, 4 with red background and 3 with black. Begin and end with a red stripe. Finish with the 6 rose panel.

On the last pattern round, dec 1 st at center back and BO the 2 steek sts. Work the last 2 rows back and forth. Finish with three-needle bind-off. Machine-stitch and cut steek. Sew down facing at lower edge. Along cut edge, pick up 4 sts (now and again 3), skip 1. Work 4 rows in stockinette and then 1 purl row on RS + 5 rows for facing. BO purlwise on RS.

Sew down facing, leaving an opening at lower edge. You'll thread a tie cord through the casing so it must be reinforced a little.

Hood used as a Cap
Casing for the cord (back): CO 5 sts. Work in stockinette over all sts to the same length as from the fold line below to the hole above. Sew this "band" up on both sides at center back. There should be an opening both above and below. Reinforce holes. Bring a cord through the casing and add a tassel to each end. It can be tightened when the hood is used as a cap.

I-cord: See Techniques. It should be as long as the casing when unstretched. First make a little pompom for one end.

Hood Lining: With Telemark and US 2 / 3 mm ndls, CO 120 sts. Work in stockinette for about 10 ¼ in / 26 cm. Steam press the hood before calculating the length of the lining; work to about ⅜-⅝ in / 1-1.5 cm from top. Continue working back and forth and then BO 2 sts at center on the next 3 RS rows. Join with three-needle bind-off (see Techniques).

Finishing
Machine-stitch, cut, and steam press lining. Bring cord through the casing on the hood, make a pompom for the other end (see above; make sure it hangs on the outside). Place lining inside hood and pin

around lower edge. Sew in lining with red yarn: split yarn and make small, even stitches. There should be an opening for the pompom. Fold the cut edge to the inside against the fold line around the face. Sew towards seam of fold line. Steam press hood and lining. If the seam at the fold line "shifts" a little, sew a little reinforcing seam inside previous seam, invisibly, of course!

Now sew on the loops around

lower edge of hood. Begin on the right side, mark placement of first loop inside the casing. The next loop should be below the 2nd "coffee bean." Now place 1 loop at every other "coffee bean" down, with the last loop at the lowest can. They will not be reverse image, because buttons are sewn in between and the loops from the neckband are here. Make the loops here a bit heavier. Sew with all plies of yarn, beginning on left side of loop, over

to the right, to the left and then right again. There will be 3 strands to sew over. Insert needle down about ⅝-¾ in / 1.5-2 cm and up again to secure the yarn and so that the loop won't distort the knitting too much. Continue as explained in the section on sewn loops in Techniques. There are a total of 7 loops.

Loops and buttons alternate below, reversed in relation to the hood so that buttons alternate buttoning from below and above. The reason for this is that otherwise there would be a line of buttons around the neckband only on one side. The hood can also be used as a cap and be buttoned to the poncho which, in turn, can be buttoned together for a little lap blanket.

The hood is wider than the neckband so it will pucker a bit between each button.
Pin the hood in place so that the casing is completely away from the buttons on the neckband when the jacket is buttoned.
Make sure the spacing from the edge is the same on both sides. First mark where the first button/loop on the neckband will be (button on the right side and loop on the left). Take the hood off again and mark even spacing for 14 buttons/loops, 7 on each side. The first button on the right side should be spaced as for the button already on the neckband, but the first loop on the left side is outside the button there. All the buttons should be parallel to these, centered on the band and relatively close together. On the left side the casing lies a little over the loop on the neckband.
After marking all the positions, sew on all the buttons for the neckband and bottom of hood. Finish by sewing the loops on neckband. These should be sewn a little below the buttons, about ⅜ in / 1 cm from the edge, and be especially well

secured. Begin on the right side, bring needle from below and up and "baste" through both layers. Sew down and up again to secure yarn to bottom layer. Sew down and up again on left side. Go down into lower layer along the loop, "baste" back to beginning and back again, then make a little stitch here (the bottom layer must be as secure as possible). Bring yarn over to the right again and sew on the loop. Make sure that all the loops are the same size and well-secured to bottom layer.
The buttons must also be well secured to the bottom layer. Buttons are all attached through two layers for extra security. Always use 2 of the 5 plies of the yarn. Sew a little back and forth on the WS so that

the button doesn't pull. Make sure that the reinforcement isn't visible and that the stitches go down well into the layers. You can also attach a small supplementary button on the back but personally I think it makes buttoning difficult.
Knit a striped I-cord for the casing. The hood can now be buttoned from each side and be used as a cap. Tighten the tip by adding a little cord with tassel. If it is too wide, it can be tightened around the face with the cord.

PONCHO/LAP BLANKET WITH HOOD/CAP

With black and US 4 /3.5 mm long circular, CO 298 sts, join, being careful not to twist cast-on row. Knit 9 rnds for facing and then

purl 1 rnd on RS for fold line. Work chart E, beginning at the arrow. The last 2 sts on the rnd are steek sts and should be worked with both yarns held together on pattern rows. The pattern is a multiple of 9 + 1 + 7 at end to balance pattern + steek = 1 + 32x9 (sts 2-10 on chart) = 289 + 7 + 2 = 298 sts around. On the side that will have a facing, you do not need to twist the yarns together; floats over 4 sts are fine. After completing panel work in MC for about 14 ½ in / 37 cm. Loosely BO the center 8 sts purlwise on RS. On next rnd, CO 4 sts over the gap. Work another 14 ½ in / 37 cm in stockinette and then BO the 2 steek sts. On the next rnd, CO 8 sts over the gap. Continue in stockinette for about 19 ¾ in / 50 cm and then work chart E, fold line and facing as at beginning of piece. BO loosely. Machine-stitch and cut along side. Sew facings down securely to WS. The panel at each side is worked back and forth. With a crochet hook, pick up sts along the side at the arrow: pick up alternately 3 and 4 sts, skipping 1 st between groups. Pick up in pattern, beginning and ending at a block (see photos).
Note: It is quite possible to pick and knit the sts with a knitting needle instead of a crochet hook but this can be difficult if the knitting is rather tight.
It can be tricky to count 4 or 3 picked up sts at the same time as maintaining the pattern stitch count. To avoid confusion, count to 4 throughout while watching the pattern. It is easy to see any mistakes.
Keep track of the stitch count. Use your right index finger to hold the sts onto the crochet hook and use another finger to hold the yarn not in use. If, in the end, the pattern doesn't come out right, you will have to rip and re-do. Trial and error! Calculate how many sts are needed for the pattern repeat and

try over one section. Space picked up sts more closely or further apart. It is better to have too few sts than too many so that the bands won't be too wide (see example F). The other side will be easier.
If necessary, put a rubber band around the end of the needle so the sts won't fall off.
Work the panel back and forth. So that one piece will be the same width as the other, purl the fold line or cut the yarn before the fold line so you can work from the opposite side. Work facing in stockinette with MC and then BO loosely. Make the panel for the other side the same way.
Machine-stitch and cut the neck opening. With black, pick up 4 or 3 sts, skip 1. Begin at front on right side and then pick up sts over the back (9) and continue to the other side. Knit back = 1 ridge. Work the front without shaping but, on every RS row, k2tog on each side of each "corner" on the back = 4 sts dec on every RS row. On the first row, k2tog tbl, k2tog, k5, k2tog tbl, k2tog. On the next row there will be 2 fewer sts between dec. Do not dec on WS rows. On the 3rd RS row, k2tog as explained and then slip the first dec st over the 2nd. Work the st reverse image at the other "corner". There should now be 1 st at center back. Knit back on WS (fold line). When working facing, inc as you had previously decreased = 1 st in each "corner" on every RS row 4 times. Make the facing about 2 rows wider than the band and then BO loosely.
Sew down facing on each side aligned with the 8 sts bound off at front. Reinforce the opening at the back with a few sts.

Tab (can be omitted)

With a crochet hook, pick up 9 sts at lower edge of neck opening on front, under the purl row. To position the yarn at the front, insert

hook at the side where picking up begins and then pick up the loose end. Knit the sts and then CO 9 new sts (see explanation for knitted button loops). Divide the sts onto 3 dpn, knit 2 rnds and then work chart G (M= Mette, worked from the top down). Knit in your own initial or a little "coffee bean." Shape tip as for a mitten top (dec as on chart G).
Sew down the back of the tab. Place the hood flat against the opening in the poncho, almost at the back. Mark spacing for loops and buttons, alternating on right and left sides. Continue the same way down the front of the poncho. When the buttons are buttoned (without the hood), you'll have a cozy little lap blanket to throw over your knees.

MITTENS

The pattern arrangements on today's mittens are often different from older mittens. Now it is common to use ribbing for the cuff. The front of the mitten often has 2 stars stacked one over the other. Older mittens often had patterns around the cuff and the pattern on the mitten itself was usually determined by the intended use, for example, as a wedding gift. The mittens might feature some wording, for example "The happy bridal pair", or a rose from the garden. Personally I prefer mittens with 2 different roses over each other, or with a star below and a smaller "round rose" above. I've knitted a mitten in this traditional style, without a narrow ribbed band. The mitten tip and thumbs are rounded and there is no increasing for a thumb gusset as for an over-mitten.

With red and dpn US 4 / 3.5 mm, CO 56 sts and work following chart H. There is no shaped thumb gusset. Knit in a strand of waste yarn to mark the thumbhole (slide sts

Note: On the chart for the thumb, the colors have been reversed. The MC (background) color for the thumb is red. This correction only pertains to the thumb chart, not the mitten hand chart!

Thumb

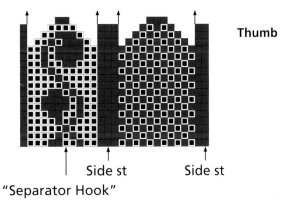

"Side st"

"Side st"

"Separator Hook"

Chart H

Left Mitten

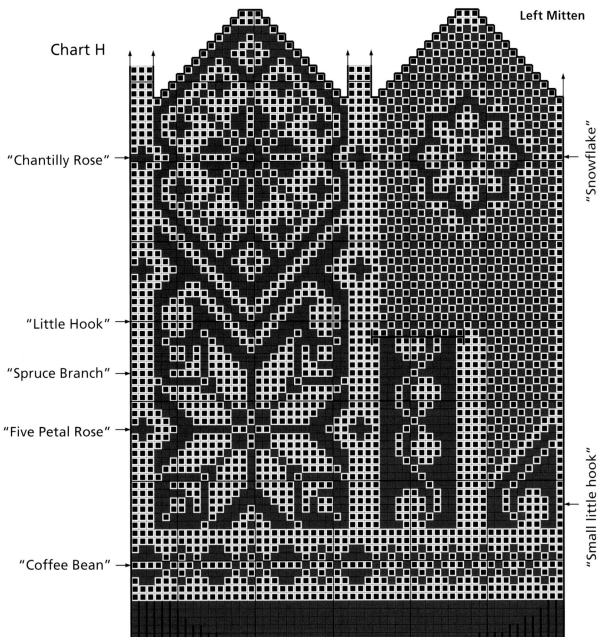

"Chantilly Rose" →

"Little Hook" →

"Spruce Branch" →

"Five Petal Rose" →

"Coffee Bean" →

← "Snowflake"

← "Small little hook"

back to left needle and knit again in pattern).

Shaping: Shape "as usual" for a mitten (following decrease lines on chart), making sure that there are 3 sts as a band at each side. On the last rnd, BO the rem 3 sts on front and back of mitten tip. Work 3 rows over one side band (3 sts) and then kitchener stitch the two bands together; stitch together any holes.

Pick out waste yarn from thumb-hole and pick up and knit 12 sts on front and 13 sts on back + 1 st at each side = 27 sts total. Make sure that the sts correspond to chart. Finish and join the 3 band sts at each side as for the mitten top. It doesn't matter if there is 1 st more on the back. When 7 sts rem, cut yarn and pull through rem sts. Weave in tails neatly on WS. Make right mitten the same way, placing thumbhole at right side of palm.

Leg Warmers

One size. Make both alike.

With black and US 4 / 3.5 mm dpn, CO 59 sts; join, being careful not to twist cast-on row. Knit facing for about 2 in / 5 cm. On the last rnd, increase 4 sts evenly spaced around to 63 sts. Make a picot fold line with CC: K1, *yo, k2tog; rep from * around. Change back to MC. Knit 5 rnds and then work stripes (chart A, repeating the 9-st pattern around), beginning at center of a "coffee bean." At the same time, on every 5th rnd, inc on each side of the 2 back center sts, to 81 sts. Work new sts into pattern. Continue to desired length. Finish with a picot rnd with CC (making small dots on each "tip").

Knit 1 rnd, and then k2tog at 8 places on rnd. Knit facing for about 2 in / 5 cm. BO as follows: k2tog, place st back on left ndl and continue as explained for sleeve top finishing in Techniques.

Autumn

Women's/Men's
Sweater/Jacket
Finnish Hood
Mittens
Ear Warmer with cross at the top (size Large)

Level of Difficulty: 2-3

Sizes	S	(M)	L	(XL)	XXL
Chest	45 ¾	(48)	50 ½	(52)	55 in
	116	(122)	128	(132)	140 cm
Length	25 ¼	(26)	26 ¾	(27 ½)	27 ½ in
	64	(66)	68	(70)	70 cm
Sleeve length	19	(19 ¼)	19 ¾	(20)	20 in
	48	(49)	50	(51)	51 cm

Yarn: Smart (100% superwash wool, 110 yds / 100 m per 50 g)

	Men's	Women's
MC	blue 5575	red 4065
CC1	red 4065	red 4109
C2	orange 3619	dark olive 9084

Yarn Amounts

Sweater	S	(M)	L	(XL)	XXL
MC	11 balls	12 balls	13 balls	15 balls	17 balls
CC1	4 balls	6 balls	8 balls	9 balls	11 balls
CC2	1 ball	1 ball	1 ball	1 ball	1 ball

Finland Hood:	Women's	Men's
MC	3 balls	3-4 balls
CC1	1 ball	1 ball

Mittens	Women's	Men's
MC	1 ball	1-2 balls
CC1	2 balls	2 balls

Ear Warmers: 2 balls MC and 1 ball CC1

Needles: US sizes 2 and 4 / 3 and 3.5 mm—dpn and long circular.

Gauge: 24 sts and 28-29 rows = 4 x 4 in / 10 x 10 cm. Adjust needle sizes to obtain correct gauge.

Notions: Men's: separating zipper, length to fit placket opening; 2 pewter buttons "Hardangar," medium. Women's: 1 pewter button, "Sissel" no. 102 and clasp no. 104.

SWEATER/JACKET

There are many possibilities for varying this garment. The charts show several alternatives for the lower body and you can choose either a stockinette or ribbed edge. Several variations of the lice pattern are also shown (see Sleeve chart). Note: On the men's model, knit 4 rounds before the lice row. That means that there are 5 rounds between each lice group. On the other models, there are 4 rounds between each lice row.
The neck opening and collar can

be varied as desired. Each of the models has a different width on the edge of the split neck. If you want a wide edging, bind off the desired number of stitches at center front and then cast on new sts for the steek, or you can machine-stitch and cut afterwards. On the women's model, the topmost part of the front motif is omitted but it is knitted on the men's model.

Body with faced edging

With CC1 and larger circular, CO 260 (271) 284 (297) 310 sts and join, being careful not to twist cast-on row. Knit about 15 rounds for the facing. On the next-to-last rnd, inc (m1 after about every 12th st) 22 (23) 24 (25) 26 sts to 282 (294) 308 (322) 336 sts total. Knit 1 more round for the facing and then either purl 1 rnd on RS for fold line or work picot edging: *k2tog, yo*; rep * to * around.

On sizes S, L, and XXL, pm around first st of rnd and the corresponding st on the opposite side = side sts. Sizes M and XL do not have single side sts. Pm around the first and last sts of rnd and the corresponding 2 sts on the opposite side. Place another color marker at center front.

Beginning at arrow for your size on chart, work chart A or B, repeating lice rows (see further details in next paragraph) and then chart C.

On size XXL, the pattern is continuous all the way around; on the other sizes, reverse pattern at sides. The lice are continuous on all sizes. Work until piece measures 11 (11 ¾) 12 ¾ (13 ½) 13 ½ in / 28 (30) 32 (34) 34 cm from fold line. Work until 4 rnds past last lice row (see chart). Work chart C.

Neck shaping: Continue straight up to desired total length, machine-stitch and cut for neck opening/placket (see section on steeks in

Lower body and sleeves, Women's

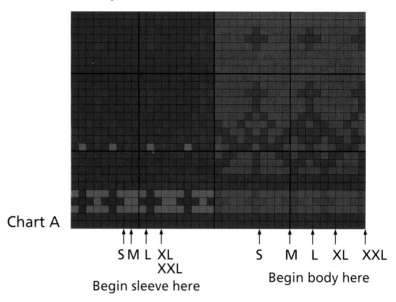

Chart A

S M L XL
XXL
Begin sleeve here

S M L XL XXL
Begin body here

Lower body and sleeves, Men's

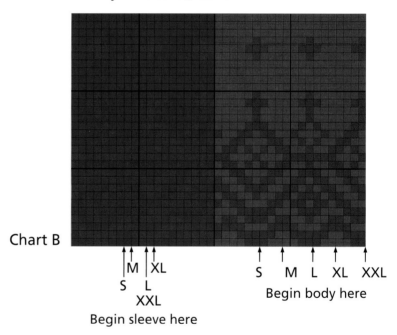

Chart B

M XL
S L
XXL
Begin sleeve here

S M L XL XXL
Begin body here

Note: Charts show alternate colorways within one chart, the designs are not intarsia. Knitter can choose desired colorway.

Techniques) or knit back and forth as shown on chart. See Finishing below for details on neck shaping and finishing.

On the men's model, the colors change a little on the top panel (see picture). BO purlwise on RS or leave sts on a holder so you can later

work three-needle bind-off (see Techniques) for shoulders.

Sleeves with faced edging

With MC and larger dpn, CO 55 (57) 61 (63) 63 sts; join to work in round. Knit 16 rnds for facing. On the next-to-last rnd, inc 8 evenly

Front Section (not back)

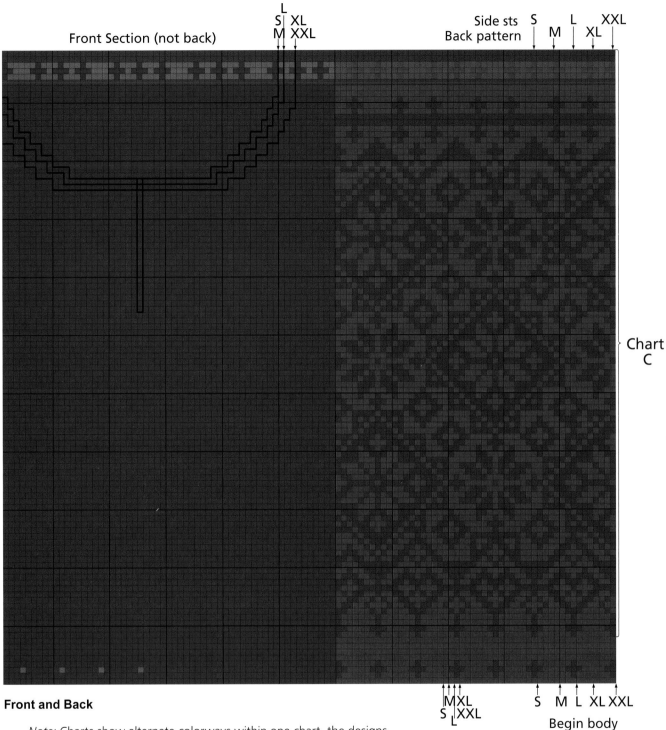

Side sts
Back pattern

Chart C

Front and Back

Note: Charts show alternate colorways within one chart, the designs are not intarsia. Knitter can choose desired colorway.

Begin sleeve

Begin body

spaced around to 63 (65) 69 (71) 71 sts. Work fold line as for body and then chart A for women's and chart B for men's sweater. Begin at arrow for sleeve and your size on chart.

Note: Panel A is a good combination with neckband chart D. When panel is almost complete (about 2 in / 5 cm), inc 1 st after first and before last st of rnd on

every 3rd rnd to 4 in /10 cm as measured from end of panel. Then inc on every 4th rnd. Work in background (lice) pattern until piece measures 10 ¼ (10 ¾) 10

Top of Sleeve

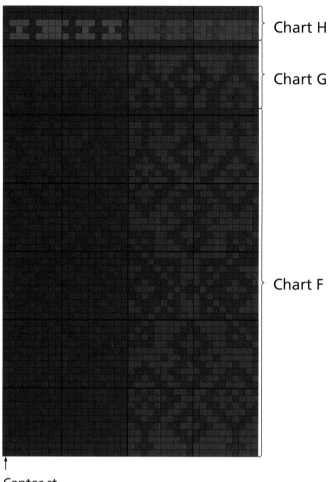

Chart H

Chart G

Chart F

↑
Center st

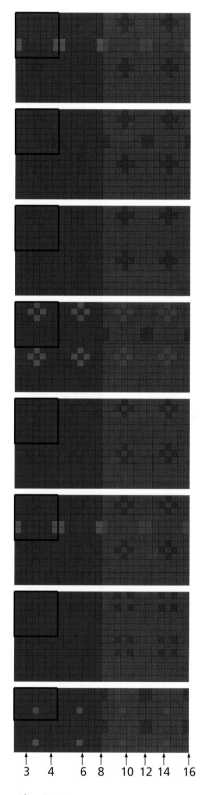

↑ ↑   ↑ ↑   ↑ ↑ ↑   ↑
3   4   6 8   10 12 14   16

Lice Pattern

¼ (10 ¾) 10 ¾ in / 26 (27) 26 (27) 27 cm (top panel measures about 8 ¾ or 9 ½ in / 22 or 24 cm). Work chart F, counting out from center st to determine where pattern begins. Sizes S and M: work chart G with CC2 as background (8 ¾ in / 22 cm). Sizes L, XL, and XXL: work charts G and H (9 ½ in / 24 cm). End with 5 rnds purl on RS for facing and then BO loosely.

Finishing
Measure top of sleeve; half the width = armhole depth. Measure depth of armhole down from shoulder seam and then machine-stitch and cut armholes. If needed, machine-stitch and cut split neck to desired length and width.
If you want a very narrow split neck edging: with desired CC, pick up

4 sts (or 3-4), skip 1 st. Pick up sts for a rounded base, making sure there is a center st at the bottom. Knit back so the "purl row" shows. Change to MC. See Techniques for how to make a narrow band edging around split neck.

If you are going to use a zipper: the space for the zipper is very narrow and you have to place it carefully so that the stitches don't slide out from it. Machine-stitch 2 rows spaced slightly apart. With CC2, pick up and knit sts and then knit back on WS (fold line), and then work facing. Increase 4 sts on each knit row so the base of the opening is rounded on the facing.

For a wider split neck edging: Begin on left side and pick up and knit

sts. Continue to base and put these sts on a holder; now pick up and knit sts along right side. Work the right side and then the left. At the base, make a small facing which is knitted downwards. Place the sts on a needle, CO 2 sts on each side and work a few rows. BO loosely and sew down facing. Choose a pattern panel or knit in a single color for the edging. If you want buttons, the sides can be the same width. Make the button loops. The buttons will then be right on the edge. You might want to make the side for the button loops a bit narrower so that the buttons will be centered on the band.

The woman's sweater is made a bit differently. Stitches are picked up and knitted around and chart J is worked around.
This will only work well when the stitch count is correct and the pattern is exactly the same on each side of the "corners." After working neckband, make a facing as explained, casting on 2 sts at each side of the little facing. Work chart K and then a single color to the center, fold line, and facing. Instead of the 2 rows with CC2, you can knit a ridge on both sides of

panel J. See pictures of the various alternatives.

Baste in zipper with 2 plies from the yarn and a thin tapestry needle. Sew the stitches straight up and down, not zigzag. Begin at bottom of one side, baste a little inside the fold line, go up and then down again, and continue on the other side. Make sure it is well-secured at base. Sew in zipper on one side, carefully stitching completely through all the layers without any thread showing on RS. Sew loosely so that the RS doesn't pull in. The top part of the zipper will be covered by the neckband. Attach a button/loop at the top. On our model has 1 button with a loop and 1 for decoration.

Neckband
With CC1, pick up and knit sts all around the neck opening, knit back so there is "bead row." Round the back edge by picking up sts down about 2 rows. Now knit chart E or J for a low edge and charts D or J + K for a bit higher neck. Make sure that the pattern is the same on both sides—count out sts from center back. On the men's model we've chosen the same panel as for

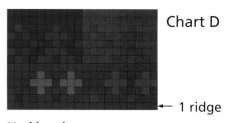

Chart D

← 1 ridge

Neckband

Chart E

← 1 ridge

Low Neckband

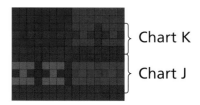

} **Chart K**

} **Chart J**

Low and High Neckbands

the top of the body. Make sure that the pattern on neckband and top of back match.
On the women's model we've made a diagonal edging at the front. Work about 4 rows in stockinette and then k2tog at beg and ssk at end of each RS row all the way up. When the band is finished, make the fold line. Begin at lower right side, pick up and knit 11 sts across diagonal, continue across band, pick up another 11 sts along diagonal on the other side. On the next row, BO 11 sts at each side, purlwise on RS. Cut yarn and continue with the facing, increasing so it will be flat. On the 2nd row, k2tog at 3 places evenly spaced across (the facing should be a bit tight). Make facing as wide as the edging and then loosely bind off purlwise on RS. Sew down facing, making sure stitching is very neat at each side. On the diagonal edge, the binding off should look like a continuation of the fold line.

**Right Mitten
2 sections**

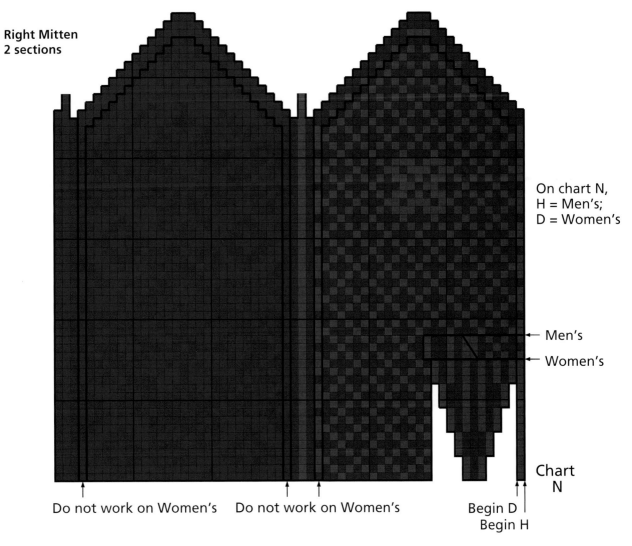

On chart N,
H = Men's;
D = Women's

← Men's

← Women's

Chart
N

↑ Do not work on Women's ↑ ↑ Do not work on Women's ↑ ↑↑ Begin D ↑
Begin H

MITTENS
Women's/Men's
With CC1 and smaller dpn, CO 48 (52) sts; join, being careful not to twist cast-on row. Work 7 rnds in stockinette for facing and then fold line (purl on RS or picot as desired); change to larger dpn and knit 1 rnd and then 1 purl rnd on RS. Work pattern on chart X, and, on the last row of men's size, dec 2 sts evenly spaced around. Continue with vertical stripes: 1 st of each color for about 6 (8) rounds—begin with MC on the right mitten and CC on the left.

Work following chart N, beginning at arrow for chosen size. Increase for thumb gusset as shown. The outermost st on the gusset should be MC; increase inside this st and knit vertical stripes above each inc. Knit in waste yarn (knit sts with waste yarn and then move them back to left needle and knit in pattern) at thumb over 11 sts for women's and 13 sts for men's. Continue and then shape top of mitten as shown on chart. Distribute sts on dpn as necessary.

Thumb
Remove waste yarn for thumb sts. Place a needle in the lower 11 (13) sts and pick up the upper 12 (14) sts. There should be 24 (26) thumb sts. For women's size pick up and knit 1 extra st and for men's k2tog on next rnd, on inside of thumb. Work stripe pattern all around,

Chart X

↑
**Begin here for
both sizes
(right mitten)**

matching stripes with outside of mitten. Work until thumb measures 2 ¼ (2 ½) in / 5 ½ (6) cm. Change to a single color and dec 8 sts evenly spaced around. Knit 2 rnds. K2tog around. Cut yarn and pull through rem sts.

Sew down facing. Make other mitten to match, placing thumbhole on opposite side of palm.

FINNISH HOOD
Women's / Men's

With collar: With MC and larger dpn or short circular, CO 216 (228) sts. Work back and forth in stockinette for 4 rows. Join and continue with 3 rnds stockinette: Shape as follows: *K16 (17), k2tog*; rep *-* around = 204 (216) sts rem. Knit 2 rnds. Working decreases over previous ones, dec on every 5th rnd (12 sts dec on each dec rnd with 1 less st between each dec) until 120 (132) sts rem = 8 dec rnds altogether. Continue as for cap without collar.

Without collar: With MC and larger dpn or short circular, CO 120 (132) sts; join to work in the round. Work in k1, p1 ribbing for about 4 in / 10 cm and then knit 2 rnds. On the next rnd, BO 15 sts at center front. Now work back and forth. At the same time, dec on each side of the opening on every other row, 2 sts 2 times and then 1 st 1 time. Work lice pattern and then shape as shown on chart M. Work until piece measures 3 ¼ (3 ½) in / 8 (9) cm from first decrease. CO 24 (21) sts over front opening. There should now be 119 (128) sts around. Cut yarn and join it again at center back and work for about 2 ¾ (3 ¼) in / 7 (8) cm after decreases, with smaller lice (1 st instead of a little cross) on every 5th rnd as before. When the space between the lice is too small, work in 1 color only. Shaping: K2tog centered between each louse, knit 5 rnds. Repeat the dec between lice and then knit 4 rnds, 2 more times. Dec and knit 3 rnds, dec and knit 2 rnds and finally, dec and knit 1 rnd. *K2, k2tog; rep from * around; cut yarn and pull through rem sts.

With desired color and larger dpn or short circular, pick up and knit sts all around opening: pick up in each st above and below; along the sides, pick up and knit 4 sts, skip 1 st across. Purl 1 rnd on RS and then knit 3 rnds; purl 1 rnd on RS (fold line). Knit facing to the same width and BO with sleeve top finishing (see Techniques) because it is the most elastic bind-off. Sew down facing.

Ear Warmer with Cross at Top
Size Large

Knit the lining first, making it tighter than the shell.

With MC and smaller dpn or short circular, CO 119 sts, join and knit 10 rnds. Place 37 sts at center front on a holder and then work back and forth for 3 rows over rem 82 sts. Dec 1 st in from edge st at beginning and end of row; work 3 rows. Rep the dec once more, work 3 rows. Place the center 22 sts on a holder. There should now be 28 sts for each ear flap. Work each side separately. Dec as before on both sections, 1 st at each side, work 3 rows. Dec 1 st on each side on every other row 4 times and on every row 2 times. This is the lining for the ear warmers. Continue, increasing as you previously decreased. When you've worked 10 increases (or when you are back to back neck), knit the 22 sts together with the earflaps on each side. Continue with the last 2 increases (on each side of the whole back part of the ear warmers) and then knit the last 37 sts on the ndl. From now on work in the round. Purl 1 rnd on RS and then knit 2 rnds. Cut yarn, and begin again at center back. Work chart L; there should be a star centered exactly over center front st. After completing panel, knit 3 rnds and then purl 1 rnd on RS. Knit about 8 rnds in stockinette (rest of lining). BO as explained in section for sleeve top finishing in Techniques. This is the most elastic finishing. Seam the "diagonal" edges neatly. Sew with RS facing; it will twist a little so that the seam shifts towards the inside. Sew in the lining all the way around. Going into the

ridge row, pick up and knit 7 sts each at front, at each side, and center back. Use a separate ball of yarn for each strap or knit them separately making sure they each have the same number of rows. Knit tightly in garter st until the pieces meet at the top, the last row should be purl on RS. Try on to make sure cap fits, stretching it just a bit. Continue around on all the "cross" sts for 1 rnd. Then *k2, k2tog; rep from * in garter st. BO. Fasten yarn, leaving a little hole at top.

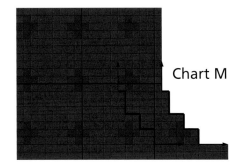

Chart M

Finnish Hood

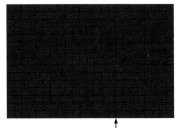

Chart L   ↑ Begin here

Ear Warmer

37

Wilderness

Pullover with stockinette or ribbed edgings; choice of patterns on the sleeves, sizes 12-XL
Hunting cap, one size
Hunting mittens and wrist warmers, women's and men's

Level of Difficulty: 2-3

Sizes	12	(14)	XS	-	S	(M)	L	(XL)
Chest	39 ¼	(41 ¼)	43 ¼	-	45 ¾	(48)	50 ½	(52 ½) in
	100	(105)	110	-	116	(122)	128	(133) cm
Length	23 ¼	(24 ½)	24 ¾	-	25 ¼	(26)	26 ¾	27 ½) in
	59	(62)	63	-	64	(66)	68	(70) cm
Sleeve length	16 ¼	(17 ¼)	18 ¼	-	19	(19 ¼)	19 ¾	(20) in
	41	(44)	46	-	48	(49)	50	(51) cm

Yarn:
Smart (100% superwash wool, 110 yds / 100 m per 50 g)

MC	CC1	CC2
gray 1053	light gray 1042	red 4038
or dark olive 9084	green 8764	light green 9544
or brown 3082	light brown 2652	rust brown 3736

Yarn Amounts

Pullover (as shown on adult models)

MC	8	9	9	-	10	11	11	12 balls
CC1	8	8	8	-	9	9	9	10 balls
CC2	1	1	2	-	1	1	1	1 balls

Pullover (as shown on children's models)

MC	8	9	9	-	10	11	11	12 balls
CC1	8	9	9	-	9	10	10	11 balls
CC2	1	1	1	-	1	1	1	1 ball

Hunting cap (1 size: large): 1 ball each MC, CC1, and CC2 + 1 ball for lining

Mittens with wrist warmers:

	Children's/Women's	Men's
MC	2 balls	2 balls
CC1	1 ball	1 ball

Needles: US size 2 and 4 / 3 or 3.5 mm—long circulars, short circulars, dpn.

Gauge: 24 sts and about 28-29 rows = 4 x 4 in / 10 x 10 cm. Adjust needle size to obtain correct gauge.

Notions: Adult jacket: 6 pewter buttons "Saga." Children's: 6 buttons "Tele."

PULLOVER

The front placket of the pullover opens so it can hang down. Make sure the buttonholes align as they can be seen from both sides.

Body with Stockinette lower edge

With MC and smaller circular, CO 220 (232) 245 – 258 (271) 284 (297) sts. Join, being careful not to twist cast-on row. Work in stockinette for approx ¾ in / 2 cm for facing. On the next rnd, inc (with m1 after approx every 12th st) 18 (20) 21 – 22 (23) 24 (25) sts evenly spaced around to 238 (252) 266 – 280 (294) 308 (322) sts. Knit 1

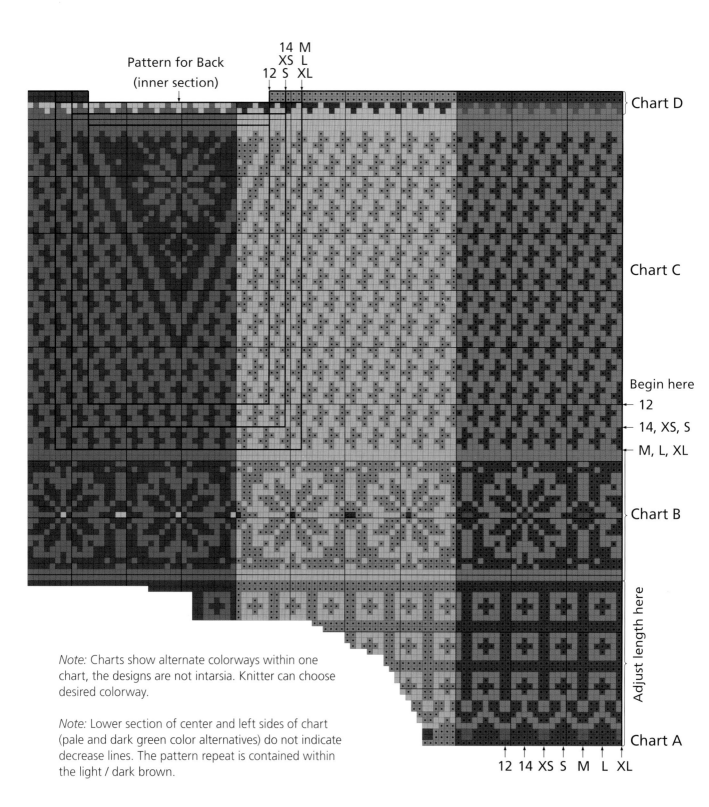

Pattern for Back
(inner section)

14 M
XS L
12 S XL

Chart D

Chart C

Begin here
← 12
← 14, XS, S
← M, L, XL

Chart B

Adjust length here

Note: Charts show alternate colorways within one chart, the designs are not intarsia. Knitter can choose desired colorway.

Note: Lower section of center and left sides of chart (pale and dark green color alternatives) do not indicate decrease lines. The pattern repeat is contained within the light / dark brown.

Chart A

12 14 XS S M L XL

rnd and then purl 1 rnd on RS (fold line). Knit 5 rnds, change to larger needles, and work pattern following chart A (see photos for arrangement of motifs).

Body with Ribbed lower edge
With MC and smaller needles, CO 208 (220) 232 – 244 (258) 270 (282) sts. Join, being careful not to twist cast-on row. Work in k1, p1 ribbing for approx 2-2 ¾ in / 5-7

cm. On the next rnd, inc (after approx every 7th st) 30 (32) 34 – 36 (36) 38 (40) sts to a total of 238 (252) 266 – 280 (294) 308 (322) sts. Knit 2 rnds in stockinette and then pm at each side and at center front

Lower Sleeve

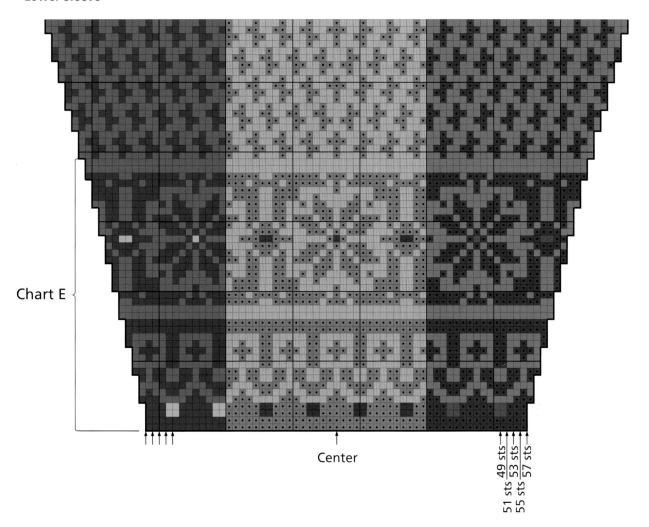

Chart E

Center

49 sts
51 sts
53 sts
55 sts
57 sts

and back. On sizes 12, XS, M and XL, pm between 2 sts at each side. On sizes 14, S, and L, pm around a side st (see arrow on chart A). Find and mark the center st of front and back. Begin knitting at arrow for desired size. See photos for arrangement of motifs.

Work straight up until piece measures 12 ¼ (13) 13 ½ - 13 ¾ (14 ¼) 14 ½ (15 ½) in / 31 (33) 34 – 35 (36) 37 (39) cm, ending as shown on chart. Pullover is now 11 (11 ½) 11 ½ - 11 ½ (12 ¼) 12 ¼ (12 ¼) in / 28 (29) 29 – 29 (31) 31 (31) cm from total length. If you need to lengthen or shorten pullover, do so now. In pattern B, there is one round with 3 colors. If that is too dif-

ficult for you to work, knit the st in the center of the star with the dark color; the sts on each side are worked in pattern color. Work chart B. Cut yarn and place 41 (47) 47 – 47 (53) 53 (53) sts at center front on a holder for neck placket. Round now begins at right front. With MC, begin pattern C at arrow for chosen size.

Note: Make sure that the pattern reverses from the sides and center back!

When you get back to center front, CO 6 sts for a steek across the sts put on holder. The center 4 of these new sts will later be the cutting line and should be knitted with both strands of yarn. The outer sts

(sts #1 and 6) should be worked in the darkest color. Continue as set. When pattern on the back is completed, begin working back and forth (this leaves a space at each side for sewing and cutting). BO the center st at each side. Now you are working on 3 separate pieces. Work the front across the full width and BO for back neck as shown on chart.

Join shoulders (make sure you have the same number of sts from back and front for shoulders) with three-needle bind-off (see Techniques).

Finishing on Front
See chart C. Three variations are shown: for sizes 12 (14, XS, S) M,

L, XL. Follow the line for your size. Place sts from holder onto needle. With the darkest yarn, work back and forth, knitting 1 garter ridge (2 rows) and then work in stockinette for about 8 rows. BO. Fold facing to WS and sew down.

With dark yarn and larger circular, pick up and knit sts from the panel and up, around the back neck and down the other side. Pick up in 6 sts and then skip 1. Make sure that each side has the same number of sts (count out from center back). Knit back (= 1 ridge) and then work the small motifs of chart D. With light yarn, work 7 (9) 11 rows in stockinette. Purl 1 row on RS for fold line. Change color and work 7 (9) 11 rows in stockinette for facing and then BO. Sew facing down around neck. Secure the edge as neatly as possible to the panel below. Now make the front placket. It can be worked in pattern or with a single dark color. In the "knots" along the edges, pick up and knit 27 (29) 31 sts. Work 33 (35) 37 rows in stockinette and then purl 1 row on RS.
With dark yarn, work 2 rows and then the little motifs of panel D (see chart). With light yarn, make facing as long as on front plus 2 rows. BO.

Now make button bands on each side of the front. Fold the fabric so it is doubled and, with light yarn, pick up and knit 6 sts for every 7 rows, going through both layers. Make sure there are 29 (30) 32 sts on each side. Work 2 (3) 4 rows in stockinette.

Now space 3 buttonholes. Buttonholes are worked over 3 sts. On all sizes, the top buttonhole is 3 sts from neck edge. Below the buttonholes should be 3 (4) 4 sts from panel.
There should be 7 (7) 8 sts between each button and the stitch count

should now be correct.

BO for each buttonhole and, on the next row, CO new sts over the gap. Knit another 3 (4) 5 rows and then purl 1 row on RS.
Make the facing the same width

as button band and don't forget to space the buttonholes as for band. Turn facing to WS and sew down. Pin the button band to the panel below and sew through all the layers. Make sure that the bands are smooth and flat. It might be a

Chart F

Top of Sleeve
(see finishing of main pattern)

Center

Chart G

Top of Sleeve
(see finishing of main pattern)

Center

bit thick here but it doesn't matter. When the front is buttoned, it needs to be rather firm.

Split yarn and sew around each buttonhole. Sew on buttons. On the children's model, we used a button with a 3-spoke pattern. It is important that all the buttons be sewn on the same way or the sweater will look messy.

Sleeves with Stockinette Cuffs
Chart E

With darkest yarn and larger ndls, CO 49 (51) 51 – 53 (53) 55 (57) sts; join, being careful not to twist cast-on row. Begin at arrow for your size on chart E. Knit 5 rnds and change to smaller ndls. Knit 6 more rnds and then purl 1 rnd on RS (fold line). Work following chart E, changing to larger ndls when pattern begins.

There are 2 center sts at underarm. Inc 1 st at each side of these sts (= 2 sts inc).

Inc on every 4th rnd a total of 9 times (up to the last pattern row of the panel).

Now inc, alternately, on every 3rd and 4th rnd until sleeve measures 9 ½ (10 ¾) 11 ½ - 12 ¼ (12 ¾) 13 (13 ½) in / 24 (27) 29 – 31 (32) 33 (34) cm. For remainder of sleeve, inc on every 3rd rnd.

When sleeve measures 12 ¼ (13 ½) 14 ¼ - 15 (15 ½) 16 (16 ¼) in / 31 (34) 36 – 38 (39) 40 (41) cm, knit top panel. Find the center st of sleeve and closely look at charts F and G. Knit the panel that most closely matches stitch count from center st.

When sleeve is complete, purl 5 rnds on RS for facing.

BO sleeve sts (see Techniques). Sew down facings on WS.

Sleeves with Ribbed edge and smaller pattern motifs

With MC and smaller ndls and dark color, CO 46 (46) 48 – 48 (48) 50 (52) sts; join, being careful not to twist cast-on row. Work in k1 tbl, p1 ribbing for 2-2 ¾ in / 5-7 cm. On the next rnd, inc 13 (15) 13 – 15 (15) 15 (15) sts evenly spaced around = 59 (61) 61 – 63 (63) 65 (67) sts. Change to larger ndls and stockinette. Inc on each side of the 2 center underarm sts on, alternately, every 3rd and 4th rnd. Begin with the first panel on chart E. To place pattern, find the center st on sleeve and count back.

Continue with main pattern (see photos for motif arrangement) until sleeve measures 9 ½ (10 ¾) 11 ½ - 12 ¼ (12 ¾) 13 (13 ½) in / 24 (27) 29 – 31 (32) 33 (34) cm. Now inc only on every 3rd rnd.

If you are working the main pattern all the way up: work until ¾ in / 2 cm from end of sleeve and then work chart D.

If you want another panel at the top of the sleeve (chart F or G), work until sleeve measures 12 ¼ (13 ½) 14 ¼ - 15 (15 ½) 15 ¾ (16 ¼) in / 31 (34) 36 – 38 (39) 40 (41) cm. Continue as explained above.

Sleeve, Finishing

Measure top of sleeve; half the width = armhole depth. Measure depth of armhole down from shoulder seam and then machine-stitch and cut armholes. Sew in sleeve from RS (see Attaching Sleeves in Techniques). Sew down facings on WS.

HUNTING CAP
One size, reversible

The cap is knitted double. It is red on one side and patterned on the other.

Shell

Choose MC—our model uses the lightest color.

With larger dpn and CC, CO 128 sts; join, being careful not to twist cast-on row. Work following chart F or G (same as for sleeve top). Continue with MC until piece measures approx 4 ¾ in / 12 cm. On the last rnd, inc 2 sts on rnd so that the decreases can be worked evenly (or you can eliminate 2 decreases on first dec rnd instead of increasing here)

Top shaping:
K8, k2tog; rep * to * around. Knit 4 rnds.
K7, k2tog; rep * to * around. Knit 3 rnds.
Continue as set with 1 less st between decreases and 2 knit rnds between each dec rnd, a total of 4 times. Now knit only 1 rnd between dec rnds. Make sure that the decreases are stacked.

Work as set until 13 sts rem, knit 1 rnd, cut yarn and pull tail through rem sts. Weave in all ends on WS.

Lining

With smaller short circular and red, pick up and knit sts through loops of cast-on row. Purl 1 rnd on RS and then work 6 rnds in stockinette. Use a long circular for knitting the last rnd (so that the ndl won't fall out).

Sew a row of chain sts over and under the little relief line (cast-on row and ridge). Sew 1 st into every knit st.

Note: This step is not necessary but it is a nice little detail. Move sts back to short circular and purl 1 rnd on RS (fold line). Change to red and knit up to beginning of decreases as for shell. Measure to be sure that the lining is the same length as shell.

Weave in all yarn tails.

Decrease as for shell. If you want a little tassel, knit an I-cord as explained in Techniques.

You can use the cap as is or add earflaps.

Ear Flaps

(not shown on models in book)
Hold the cap with the red side in-

side. With dark yarn and larger dpn, pick up and knit sts through both layers, 1 row inside the fold line. CO the same number of sts on inside for other side of flap. Knit around for about 1 ½ in / 4 cm and then decrease in each side as for tip of a mitten (on each side: ssk, knit to last 2 sts, k2tog): dec on rnd 1, knit 1 rnd without decreasing. Now dec on every rnd for about 8-10 rnds or to desired length. BO. Weave in ends on WS. Neatly sew opening at lower edge.

Pin CO edge to red side, and carefully sew with split yarn. To hide this seam, sew over it with a row of chain sts all around the cap. Sew with dark yarn and make sure that it is not visible on the other side. Sew 1 st in each knit st, being careful not to pull in cap.

HUNTING MITTENS

Mittens and Wrist Warmers in one. You can also make these as regular mittens.

For our model, the darkest color is MC.

With larger dpn, and MC, CO 55 (63) sts, join, and work in garter st for 8 rnds. Knit the next rnd and inc 1 st to 56 (64) sts. Work chart H for children's/women's and chart I for men.

After completing pattern, knit 1 rnd and then a dec rnd: dec 14 (16) sts evenly spaced around to 42 (48) sts. Work in k1, p1 ribbing for 8 rnds and then knit 1 rnd.

Work chart K for children's size and J for women's / men's.

Note: For men's size, inc 2 sts on each side of mitten: 2 sts on side of the chart and 2 sts at center, see arrows on chart. Make sure that the stars are centered above the stars of cuff (follow center st down).

Inc for thumb gusset as shown on chart. Place the 11 (13) sts of thumb gusset on a holder. CO 11 (13) new sts over gap with MC (cut CC). Knit 0 (1) more rnd. On the

Chart J

Mitten— women's/men's

+2 men

+2 men

Center

Men
Women

Thumb

-2 children's   -2 women's/children's

Center

Chart I

Mitten pattern for men

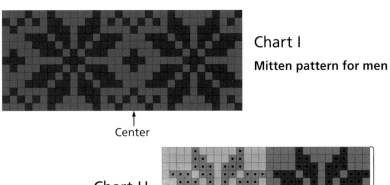

Chart H

Mitten pattern for women/children's

x 2

Center

next rnd, knit with waste yarn over 25 (27) sts on palm of mitten (see chart). Continue (beginning with sts on waste yarn) pattern as set and shape top as shown on chart. On women's size, the decreases begin 2 rnds sooner than shown on chart (follow chart J at this point). There should be 2 sts between dec sts. On men's size, dec with 4 sts between decreases.

Thumb

Place thumb gusset sts on dpn and pick up 11 (13) sts from cast-on. For women's, eliminate 2 sts on inside of thumb. The women's thumb is also a bit shorter than shown on chart. For children's size, omit 2 sts each on inside and outside of thumb = 4 sts less.

Note: If you want the thumb to be free to lift off, CO sts on the inside instead of picking them up.

Work thumb as charted. For children's/women's, knit 2 rnds fewer than shown on chart (see bracket) and then shape as shown.

Hand flap

Remove waste yarn and place sts from lower edge on a holder. On the top side, pick up and knit between sts = 26 (28) sts. Work flap back and forth in stockinette with one color, always knitting the first 2 sts on each side (= garter edges). With MC, begin on side opposite thumb and work 1 row. BO 11 sts purlwise over thumb, p1, stockinette until 2 sts rem, k2. Now k2tog at beginning and end of every WS row until 6 (7) sts rem inside the 2 edge sts at each side. Work another 5 (7) rows, decreasing until there are 2 (3) sts. Now increase to 6 (7) sts and BO.

Fold at narrowest point and sew down smoothly around, using split yarn and fine sts. Sew in a large snap inside the flap.

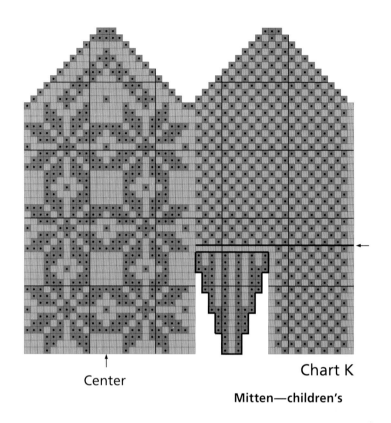

Chart K

Mitten—children's

Center

Fingers

With MC, CO 25 (27) new sts and knit around in stockinette for about 1 ¼-1 ½ in / 3-4 cm, until you reach base of little finger. Begin from same side as index finger. Now knit 1 rnd, except for 6 sts of back of hand and 6 sts of palm (for little finger). CO 1 st between omitted sts. Place sts for little finger on a holder.

Index finger:
Knit with the last 7 (8) sts from back of hand and the next 6 (7) sts from the palm; CO 2 new sts between these = a total of 15 (17) sts. Knit 8 rnds and then bind off as for sleeve top finishing (see Techniques).

Middle finger:
Knit 7 (8) sts from back of hand and the next 6 (7) sts from palm; CO 2 sts between them facing ring

finger. Pick up 1 st from cast-on for index finger = a total of 16 (18) sts. Knit 8 rnds and BO as for index finger.

Ring finger:
Knit with the last 13 sts of hand. Pick up and knit 1 (2) sts from middle finger CO = a total of 14 (15) sts. Knit 7 rnds and then BO as for index finger.

Little finger:
Knit the 12 sts on holder and pick up and knit 1 st from ring finger CO. Knit 5 (6) rnds and BO. Sew the finger section securely to inside of mitten and sew on other half of snap.

The Norwegian

Men's Pullover, sizes XS-XL
Hood/cap, lined, one size

Level of Difficulty: 3

Sizes	XS	(S/M)	L	(XL)
Chest	39 ½	(46)	49 ¼	52 ½) in
	100	(117)	125	(133) cm
Length	25 ¼	(26)	26 ¾	(27 ½) or longer in
	64	(66)	68	(70) or longer cm
Sleeve length,	19	19 ¼)	19 ¾	(20) in
Ribbed cuff	48	(49)	50	(51) cm
Sleeve length,	17 ¾	(18 ½)	19 ¼	(19 ¾) in
Stockinette cuff	45	(47)	49	(50) cm
and buttons				

Yarn: Smart (100% superwash wool, 110 yds / 100 m per 50 g)
MC: black 1099
CC1: red 4219
CC2: green 8764
CC3: yellow 2417
CC4: dark red 4065

Yarn Amounts:
Sweater

MC	10	11	12	13 balls
CC1	7	8	8	9 balls
CC2	2	2	2	2 balls
CC3	1	1	1	2 balls
CC4	1	1	1	1 ball

Cap, lined (1 size: large): 2 balls each MC and CC1 + 3-4 balls for lining

Needles: US size 4 / 3.5 mm – long and short circulars, dpn. US size 2 or 3 / 3 mm short circular for stockinette sleeve cuff finishing.

Gauge: 24 sts and 28-29 rows = 4 x 4 in / 10 x 10 cm. Adjust needle size to obtain correct gauge.

Notions: Neckband: 2 pewter clasps and 1 button "Bjørg." Sleeve cuffs: 4 pewter buttons "Bjørg." Cap: 2 pewter buttons "Bjørg."

PULLOVER
Body with ribbed lower edge
With MC and long circular, CO 238 (257) 275 (293) sts; join, being careful not to twist cast-on row. Work in k1tbl/p1 ribbing for 2 (2 ½) 2 ½ (2 ¾) in / 5 (6) 6 (7) cm. On the last rnd, inc 22 (23) 25 (27) sts with m1 after about every 11th st to a total of 260 (280) 300 (320) sts. Pm at each side st and center front and back sts. Work pattern A, making sure it matches at marked sts. Continue with either one of the lice patterns or a single color. Begin lice pattern at arrow for your size. Work until piece measures 13 (13 ¾) 14 ¼ (15) in / 33 (35) 36 (38) cm (the lice pattern measures 12 ¼-12 ¾ in / 31-32 cm). The center pattern on chart B can be worked on the front, followed by charts C and D. *Note on chart D:* Always work the single color rnds with MC and make

a garter ridge = knit 1 rnd, purl 1 rnd. After the last ridge, place the center front 48 sts on a holder. On the next rnd, CO 4 new sts over the gap for the steek. Work steek sts throughout as: 1 st with MC, 2 sts with both yarns, 1 st with MC. Continue with charts E and F. The large star is knitted only on the back.

Work the last 4 (5) 7 (7) rows back and forth to allow for a little "work space" for sewing and cutting. On the last row, BO 48 (50) 52 (54) sts at center back and 4 (6) 8 (10) sts at center front = 41 (45) 49 (53) sts rem for each shoulder. Join shoulders with three-needle bind-off (see Techniques).

Body with stockinette lower edge

With MC and long circular, CO the same number of sts as for body with ribbed lower edge. Knit 12 rnds for a facing and then inc with m1 after about every 11th st to 260 (280) 300 (320) sts. Make picot edge for fold line: *k2tog, yo*; rep * to * around. Knit 3 rnds and then work pattern L. Knit 2 rnds with MC and finish with chart K (see photo for pattern arrangement). Continue to desired length minus 12 ¼-12 ¾ in / 31-32 cm. Now continue as for body with ribbed lower edge, first working in lice pattern for 12 ¼-12 ¾ in / 21-32 cm.

Sleeves with ribbed cuffs

With MC and dpn, CO 48 (50) 52 (54) sts; join to work in the round. Work in k1tbl/p1 ribbing for 2 ½-2 ¾ in / 6-7 cm. On the last rnd, inc 15 (17) 19 (19) sts evenly spaced around to 63 (67) 71 (73) sts. Work chart K and then continue in your choice of lice pattern. *At the same time*, inc 1 st at underarm (after first st and before last st) on every 4th rnd. Work new sts into pattern. Work in lice pattern until sleeve measures approx 8 ¼ (8 ¾) 9 (9

½) in / 21 (22) 23 (24) cm. End as shown on chart. Complete charted rows for sleeve = 10 ¾ in / 27 cm. *Note:* on the smaller sizes, you may wish to knit fewer patterns, so you could omit chart G, for example. In that case, make sure that all measurements are correct.

After the last rnd with MC, knit 5 rnds in reverse stockinette for facing. BO with sleeve top finishing (see Techniques).

Sleeves with stockinette cuffs and buttons

With MC and dpn, CO 60 (62) 64 (68) sts; divide sts onto 4 dpn and join to work in the round. *Knit 1 rnd, purl 1 rnd*; work * to * a total of 3 times = 3 ridges. Now work following chart J. On the 2nd rnd with MC, inc 1 st on every dpn (= 4 sts increased on rnd) = 64 (66) 68 (72) sts. Work charts D and K. *At the same time*, inc 2 sts on every 4th rnd as for sleeves with ribbed cuffs. Work new sts into pattern. From this point on, work as for sleeves with ribbed cuffs.

Finishing

Measure top of sleeve. Half of width = depth of armhole. Measure down from shoulder to armhole depth and then machine-stitch and cut armhole; attach sleeves (see Attaching Sleeves in Techniques).

Front Placket

Place front sts on ndl and CO 1 new st at each side. Work in stockinette for a facing the same width as

Lower body with ribbing

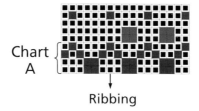

Chart A { Ribbing

Back Patterns

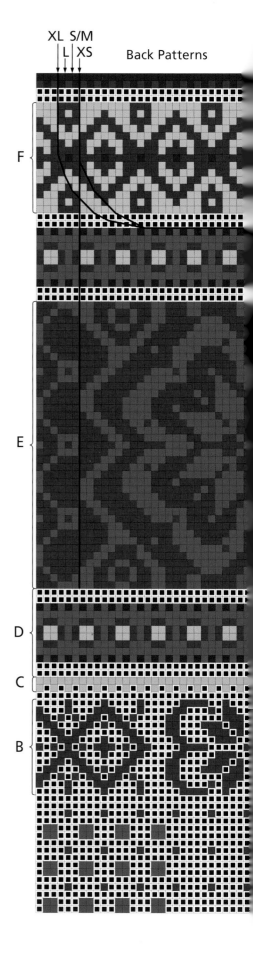

XL S/M
L XS

F

E

D

C

B

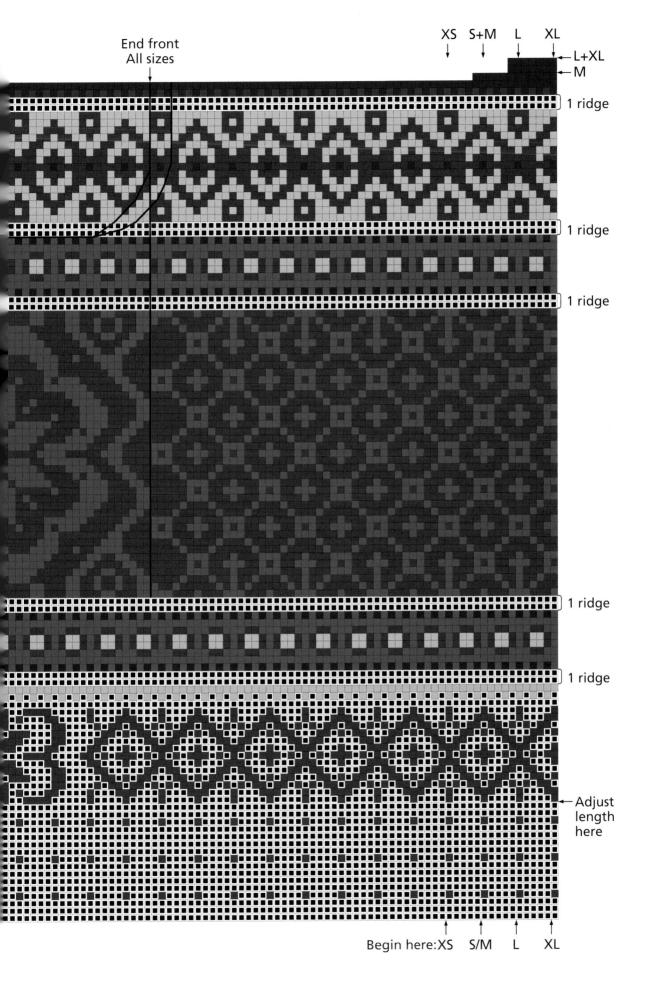

End front
All sizes

XS S+M L XL
← L+XL
← M

1 ridge

1 ridge

1 ridge

1 ridge

1 ridge

← Adjust
   length
   here

Begin here: XS S/M L XL

panel D. Fold facing down and sew down on WS.

With MC and RS facing, pick up and knit approx 43 (44) 45 (46) sts on one side of front in the knit sts straight down along the pattern (pick up 5 sts for every 6 rows). CO 1 extra st at base. Count so you can make sure you have the same number of sts on each side. Begin at bottom with pattern M. The pattern should look as if it continues directly from the panel below. Shape neck by binding off 4-3-2-2-1 sts at neck edge on every other row. Work with MC to center front (knitting a bit tighter with the single color). Purl 1 row on RS for fold line and then continue in stockinette for facing. Inc as you had decreased before. Work a couple of extra rows on facing so it won't be too thick at seamline. BO loosely. Fold placket at fold line and sew down as smoothly and invisibly as possible. Work other side of placket the same way.

Neckband

With MC, pick up and knit approx 127-133 sts around neck. On the larger sizes, pick up 1-2 sts inside the edge (see arrow on chart). Pick up and knit sts evenly down to neck placket, pick up through both layers and make sure both sides have the same number of sts. Count forward from center back to make sure stitch counts match those of pattern.

Work panel M. Work only 2 rows with MC and then make picot fold line: *k2tog, yo*; rep * to * around. Work facing as wide as panel on smaller needles. BO loosely purlwise on RS.

Edging with buttonholes on stockinette cuff sleeves

Edging is worked from the front to the back.

Right sleeve: Pm at center of sleeve cuff. Insert yarn end with a tapestry

needle 1 st past where the last st will come (lowest edge). Use this yarn tail from the back of the work. Knit up st (in the same line from the ridge to ridge, from above and down) with MC and smaller ndls, pick up and knit 4 sts for every 5 rows. The yarn is now on RS. Knit 1 row back (= 1 ridge) and then work 5 rows in stockinette + 1 purl row on RS for fold line. Work facing with 1 row less than edging; BO. Left sleeve: Insert needle from the top and pull through as much yarn as needed for picking up sts. Pick up towards yarn tail. The ridges can be knitted instead of purled. Fold edge under and sew down smoothly. Sew on 2 loops with buttonhole st along the fold line. Sew buttons to back on the sleeve so that the cuffs are tight enough when buttoned. A supplementary button on the back works well.

Lined Hood/Cap

Use a 20 in / 50 cm circular and work back and forth.
With MC, CO 13 sts, knit back and then CO 4 new sts; turn.
Purl back and CO 4 new sts; turn. Continue in stockinette and work 2 more rows with 4 new sts on each; turn = 29 sts.
Add lice color and work *K4 MC, k1 lice*; continue row, CO 3 new sts; turn.
On the next row, knit the first st with both colors held together (to secure the lice yarn, it will be hidden in the facing later).
Finish row and CO 7 new sts = 39 sts. Cut MC and slide sts down needle. With RS of first ear flap facing, begin other ear flap on the same needle. With MC, CO 13 sts. Knit these sts and then (CO 4 new sts) 2 times at each side = a total of 4 more times = 29 sts; turn.
K4 MC, k1 lice, CO 4 new sts; turn. Work back and CO 3 new sts; turn. From this point, work both pieces together, making sure that the

Sleeve with ribbed cuffs

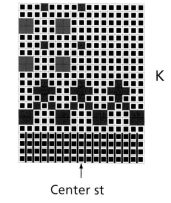

K

Center st

Sleeve with stockinette cuffs and buttons

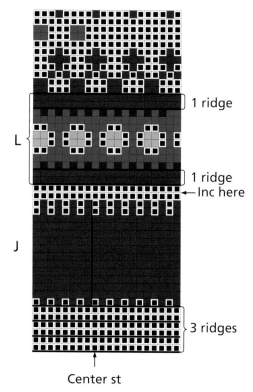

1 ridge

L

1 ridge
← Inc here

J

3 ridges

Center st

pieces are arranged correctly on ndl. Continue working back and forth. Now CO 2 new sts at end of every row a total of 5 times at each side. *At the same time*, continue knitting in lice on every 5th row. Knit the lice yarn with MC on the first st on the side where the yarn tail hangs. Finally, CO 3 new sts 2 times at each side plus only 3 sts at the end of the last knit row = 110 sts. Cut yarn. Attach yarn at center back st (centered between 2 lice). This is now beg of rnd.

CO 30 new sts between the two sections = 140 sts. Now join to work in the round and knit 2 rnds, then a lice rnd. Continue alternating 1 lice with 2 MC rnds.

Work panel B (see sweater chart). Work only the diamond motif of chart B around (multiple of 10 sts), not the front motif (see photo). After completing panel B, work 3 rnds and then begin shaping: K1, *k2tog, k23, ssk*; rep from * to * around. Knit 1 rnd without decreasing. Continue decreasing on every other rnd with 2 fewer sts between decreases each time (see chart N). Work in pattern or a single color. After last charted rnd, cut yarn and pull tail through rem sts; weave in all tails neatly on WS. Make lining as for cap in a single color. Use smaller ndls or knit more tightly with fewer rows. Try on to make sure lining fits inside cap well.

Finishing

With same yarn color as for lice, pick up and knit in the sts worked with two strands so that unevenness at the edge can be hidden. Make sure lice are spaced equally on right and left sides. Work 4 rnds in stockinette and then a fold line: purl 1 rnd on RS.

Work 2 rnds as: *K1 MC, k1 lice color*; rep * to * around and then knit 2 rnds with lice color. BO loosely. Pin lining to cap and then sew around edges, making sure sts are invisible on RS.

Try on the cap and mark the sides of each ear. Sew a button onto each side with a supplementary button on the inside. Twist or knit 2 cords, making a loop for a buttonhole on one side of each cord. Attach button to each cord. The cords normally tie at the back of the head but can also be tied under the chin when it is windy.

Sleeve, Top

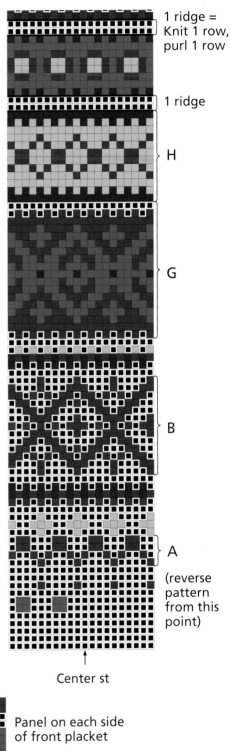

1 ridge =
Knit 1 row,
purl 1 row

1 ridge

H

G

B

A

(reverse
pattern
from this
point)

↑
Center st

Cap, Top Shaping

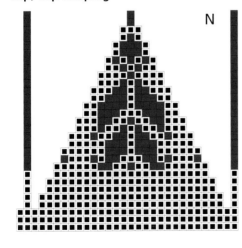

N

Neckband

1 ridge

Panel on each side
of front placket

1 ridge

M

↑
1 extra st at
lower edge

Moose

Sweater/Jacket, sizes 14-XL
Patterned Cap with tassel, women's/men's
Patterned Cap, all sizes
Half Gloves, women's/men's

Level of Difficulty: 3

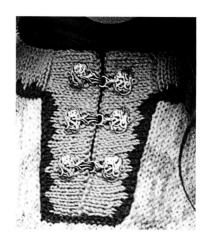

Sizes	14	(S)	M	(L)	XL
Chest	41 ¾	(45)	48	(51 ¼)	54 ¼) in
	106	(114)	122	(130)	138 cm
Length	26	(27 ¼)	28 ¼	(28 ¼)	29 ¼ in
	66	(69)	72	(72)	74 cm
Sleeve length	17 ¼	(18 ¼)	18 ½	(19 ¾)	20 ½ in
	44	(46)	47	(50)	52 cm

Yarn:
Peer Gynt (100% wool, 98 yds / 91 m per 50 g)

		Women's	Men's
MC	moss 2063	white 1012	brown 3082/3094
CC1	brown 3082	beige 2622	beige 2652
CC2	mustard 2346	rust 3736	rust 3736
CC3	yellow 2323	dark red 4049	dark red 4049

Smart can be substituted but you should knit next larger size and check measurements.

Yarn Amounts
Jacket (yarn amounts calculated for jacket with 2 border panels)

MC	8	9	9	10	11 balls
CC1	26	27	28	29	30 balls
CC2	1	1	1	2	2 balls
CC3	2	2	2	3	3 balls

Patterned Cap with tassel: 1 ball of each color
Patterned Cap: 1 ball of each color
Wrist Warmers: 1 ball MC and small amounts of CC colors

Needles: US sizes 2 and 4 (or 6 if necessary for gauge) / 3 and 3.5 (or 4.0) mm. – long and short circulars, dpn.

Gauge: 22 sts and approx 27 rows = 4 x 4 in / 10 x 10 cm. Adjust needle size to obtain correct gauge.

Notions: Jacket: 3 pewter buttons "Drage."

SWEATER/JACKET
At first glance, this pattern looks very complicated, but, actually it is fun to knit and you'll quickly learn the pattern. The main problem is beginning at the correct place. I measured out 4 in / 10 cm of the moose motif and began where one was placed on a panel and then knitted 2 motifs. Since this is how it should have looked, it must have been completely correct. It would not have been a big problem, anyway, because I could have ended it correspondingly earlier.
The chart shows all the combinations of sizes with 1 or 2 wide panels.

Norwegian Patterns for Knitting corrections-

Page 54

Moose: Yarn amounts

14 S M L XL

MC: 8 9 9 10 11 balls

CC 1: 7-8 8 8 9 10 balls

CC 2: 1 1 1 2 2 balls

CC 3: 2 2 2 3 3 balls

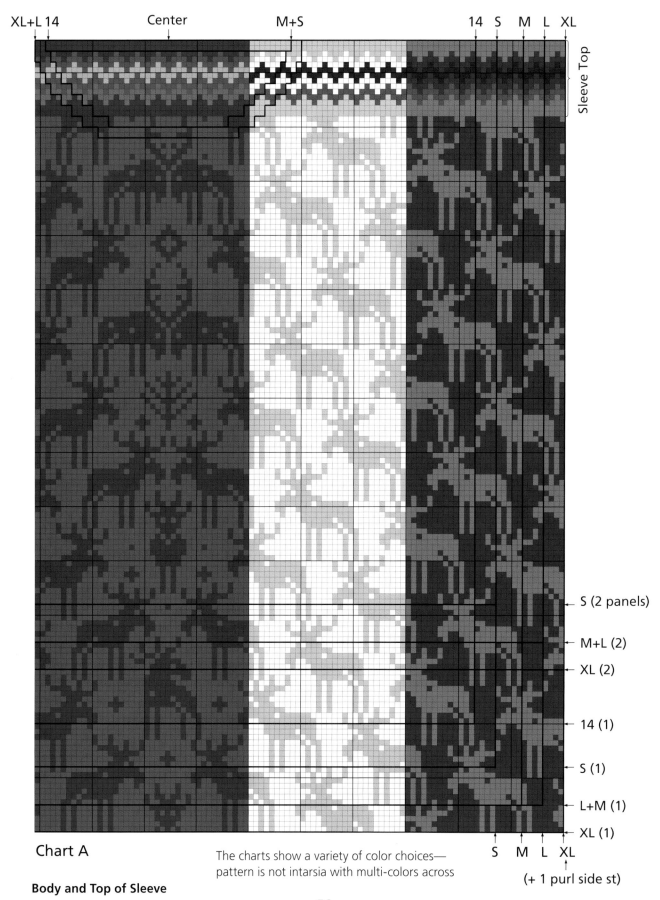

Chart A

Body and Top of Sleeve

The charts show a variety of color choices—
pattern is not intarsia with multi-colors across

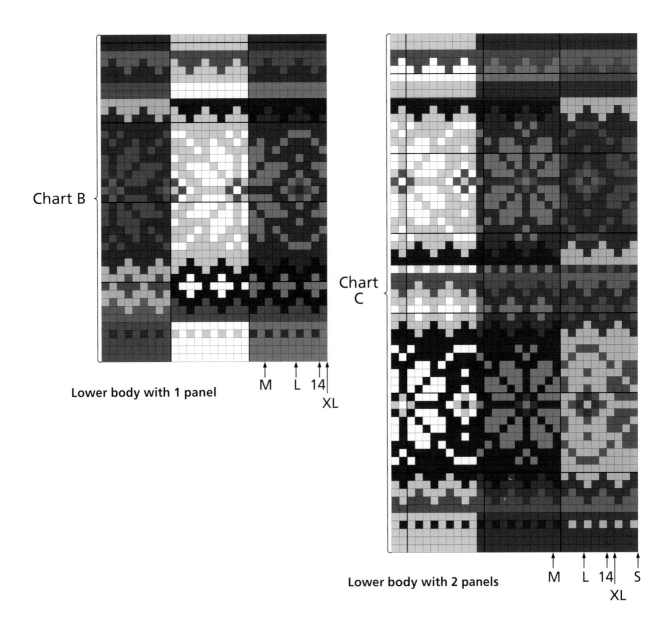

Chart B

Chart C

Lower body with 1 panel

M   L   14|
         XL

Lower body with 2 panels

M   L   14| S
         XL

Draw a pencil line on the chart for size desired (it can be erased later). The numbers in parentheses to the right of the chart show how many panels to make at the lower edge. The panels are somewhat different for women's and men's sizes (see charts B and C). If you want a shorter sweater, knit a narrower border at lower edge. You can use the narrow sleeve panel or 1 wide panel and then follow the chart for as many rows as you want. Choose whichever of the several color variations you like.

Body
Model with 1 lower panel:
With MC and larger circular, CO 220 (235) 254 (296) 284 sts; join, being careful not to twist cast-on row. Work in stockinette for 2-2 ¾ in / 5-7 cm. On next-to-last rnd, inc with m1 after about every 14th st to 236 (252) 272 (288) 304 sts. Purl 1 rnd on RS for fold line. Work chart B.

Model with 2 lower panels:
With MC and larger circular, begin as for model with 1 lower panel and knit facing. Instead of purl rnd,

work picot fold line: *K2tog, yo*; rep * to * around. Change to CC1 and work chart C.

Model with narrow panel:
With CC1 and larger circular, begin as for model with 1 lower panel and knit facing, increase, and purl fold line. Work as much as you want of the wider panels or a narrow panel such as on sleeves.

All variations:
Knit 2 rnds. On the last rnd, k58 (62) 67 (70) 75, pm around next st for center front. Knit same number

57

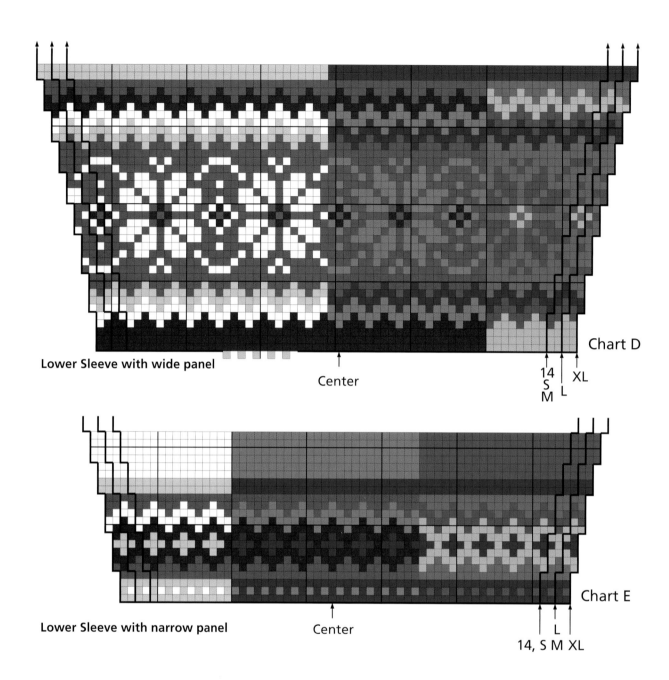

Lower Sleeve with wide panel

Center

14
S
M

L

XL

Chart D

Lower Sleeve with narrow panel

Center

14, S M XL

L

Chart E

of sts as before marker, pm at sides, center back, and last st on rnd. Use a different color marker for each place. Move markers up on each rnd.

Now work following chart A, always purling each side st with MC.

Split Neck

Decide how deep you want the split neck, making sure it won't cut into a moose. BO 13 sts at center front

(see binding off for buttonholes in Techniques) and CO 4 new sts over gap on next row. Always work these 4 steek sts with both strands of yarn.

BO for neck (see chart) and work back and forth or continue in the round. If working straight up, BO 45 (47) 47 (51) 51 sts at center front and back (see Techniques). Join shoulders with three-needle bind-off (see Techniques).

On the last pattern rnd, BO purl sts at each side and work the 2 last rows back and forth – this makes a little space for sewing and cutting later. Fold facing to WS and sew down.

Sleeves

Chart AA shows the left sleeve. With same ndl size (dpn or short circular) as for body and MC, CO 56 (56) 56 (60) 60 sts and join to

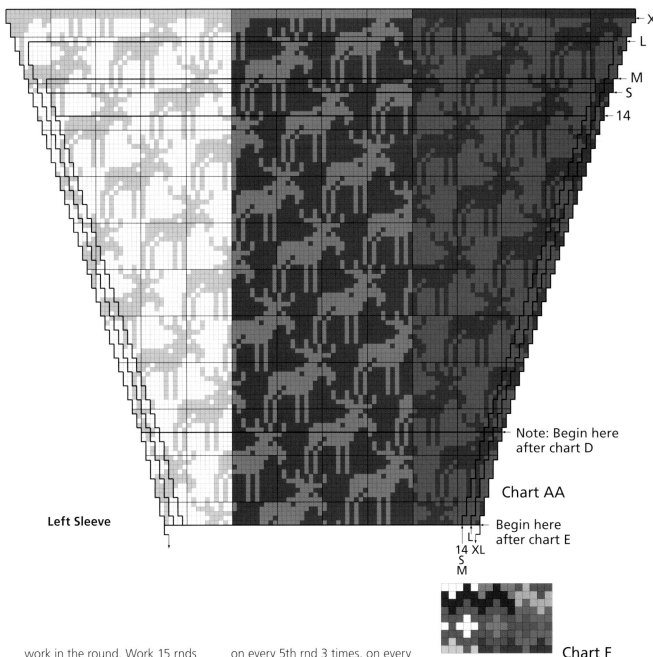

XL

L

M

S

14

Note: Begin here
after chart D

Chart AA

Begin here
after chart E

14 XL
S
M

Left Sleeve

Chart F

Round Neckband

work in the round. Work 15 rnds in stockinette for facing. On the 5th and 10th rnds, dec 1 st at each side of center st (underarm). On the next-to-last rnd, inc 4 sts evenly spaced around. Work following chart for either panel D or E. Make sure that you begin at the correct place for the panel. For the wide panel, begin at the marked line.

Inc on each side of the underarm st on every 5th rnd 3 times, on every 4th rnd to "Note" and then on every 3rd rnd.

When working the horizontal panels, work the underarm st in pattern. On the moose pattern purl the underarm st with MC up to the last panel. This is the last st on the left side of each chart. Work moose motif until 2 in / 5 cm from total sleeve length. Finish with the same panel as for upper body.

Finish with 5 purl rnds on RS. On the smallest size, inc 2 sts on the 3rd rnd of the facing so that it will stretch easily around the armhole. Work the facing back and forth. BO as for sleeve finishing (see Techniques).

Work the other sleeve in reverse image. Unfortunately I forgot to do this on one section.

Neck Finishing

Machine-stitch and cut neck opening, following chart for shaping. Pin baste or machine baste and stitch just inside basting line. Machine-stitch and cut split neck at front.

Round neck

With CC1, pick up and knit sts around neck, beginning at one shoulder. If you didn't sew and cut a shaped back neck, pick up sts in a shallow curve over about 2-4 rows (otherwise the back neck won't be long enough). Make sure you pick up a multiple of 4 sts and that the pattern matches at each side and with the pattern below neck. Count out sts from center front and back and make sure the stitch count is correct. Purl 1 rnd on RS, knit 1 ridge, and then panel F. When the panel is complete, knit 1 rnd and purl 1 rnd on RS (fold line). Knit the facing with smaller needles and bind off as for sleeve finishing (see Techniques). It is important that the neckline be flexible enough to fit over the head. Sew down facing.

Finishing Jacket with split neck

With color of your choice, pick up and knit 15 sts at lower edge of split neck (on the model, we've used CC3). Knit back = 1 ridge. On the next row, CO 2 new sts at beginning and end of row and knit across. Change to MC and continue in stockinette for a ¾ in / 2 cm facing; BO.

Pick up and knit sts around the neck with the same color as for lower edge of split neck, making sure that the sections match at both sides. If you want, pick up sts in a shallow curve over about 2-3 rows so the back neck won't be too long. Because this is a jacket you could also pick up sts straight across. Knit back = 1 ridge. Make sure that the ridge is not knit too loosely. Count sts from center back. The pattern is a multiple of 4 and should match the pattern on the back.

Work small points in pattern: 3 sts with CC3 and 1 st with CC1, then 1 st with CC3 and 3 sts with CC1 (see model). The rest of the neck band is worked in a single color.

Note: Leave a tail of about 11 ¾ in / 30 cm in CC1 to use later.

Work 7 rows and then purl 1 row on RS (fold line). On the 2nd row of facing, dec 1 st at each shoulder. Work facing with smaller needles to same width as edge. BO as for sleeve top finishing (see Techniques). Sew down facings with split yarn.

Bands

Right band: Begin with CC3 to pick up and knit below as a continuation of the ridge. Pick up 3 sts for every 4 rows.

Pick up to the ridge around the neck and then continue with the yarn tail of CC1. Purl back over the neck edge and then continue with CC3 but knit so that there is a ridge below. Begin to count sts at the top; the pattern should be a continuation of the neckband pattern. Work down and then back up, making sure that the band is smooth.

If this is too hard, the band will be nice with just garter st and not a pattern at the sides. Work in one color at the top near the neck (see photo).

Work until band is as wide as half of split neck, purl 1 row on RS for fold line and then knit facing. The facing can be about ⅜ in / 1 cm wider than the band. If you are using clasps, the band must be reinforced.

Left band: Begin at top with CC1 and pick up and knit sts down to the ridge, let tail hang. Continue with CC3, picking up as many sts as for the other side. Knit back for a ridge and then purl with CC2; turn and knit down again. Work in pattern as for right side.

Continue as for right band.

Sew down all facings with split MC yarn. Sew the top with CC1 (this makes it look nice when the jacket is open at neck).

Sew on pewter clasps making sure that the clasps come in at the points in the pattern panel. Sew with 2 strands of yarn.

Sleeve Finishing

Measure top of sleeve; half the width = armhole depth. Measure depth of armhole down from shoulder seam and then machine-stitch and cut armholes (see Techniques). Sew down from the small holes– that will be sufficient…

Attach sleeve from RS with 1 st in each knit st inside the machine-stitch line of the body. Sew into the lowest ridge of the purl rnd of sleeve. Sew the facing over cut edge on WS (with split thread). Sew down facing at sleeve cuffs.

CAP WITH PATTERN PANELS AND POMPOM

Women's / Men's

In order for the stitch count to be a multiple of 16, knit the smallest cap loosely and the largest tightly. Choose your own colors – three variations are shown on the chart. The MC should be the color you have the most of (for facing). With MC and needles for desired gauge, CO 103 (117) sts; join to work in the round. Work in stockinette for about 4 ¼ in / 11 cm. On the next

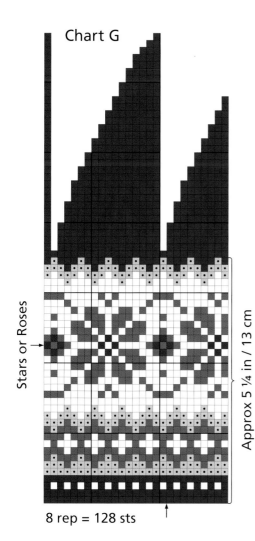

Chart G

Stars or Roses

8 rep = 128 sts

Top shaping for cap with panel and pompom

Approx 5 ¼ in / 13 cm

Chart K

Patterned Cap

rnd, inc after about every 11th st with m1 to 112 (128) sts. Knit 1 rnd. Change to the color that will make small dots at the fold line: *yo, k2tog*; rep * to * around. Change to desired colors and work following chart G, beginning at arrow. There are 7 (8) pattern rep around. After working panel, knit 1 rnd and then shape top as follows:
K2tog, k14; rep * to * around. Knit 3 rnds.
K2tog, k13; rep * to * around. Knit 2 rnds.
K2tog, k12; rep * to * around. Knit 2 rnds.
Now dec on every other rnd with 1

st less between dec until 8 sts rem. Cut yarn and bring through rem sts. Make one large or several small pompoms on cords or leave cap as is. Sew down facing on WS.

Thread twisted cord through holes at bottom edge if desired.

If you want a "rounder" cap, stop decreasing when the cap is long enough, k2tog around 2 times with 1 rnd between dec rnds. Cut yarn and pull through rem sts; pull tight. Attach a large pompom.

Cap with Overall Pattern

CO a multiple of 4, join and work around in stockinette for 1 ½ in / 4 cm for facing. Inc 8 sts evenly spaced around and knit 1 more rnd. Purl 1 rnd on RS for fold line and then work following chart K. Work to desired length and finish pattern. Work 1 rnd k2tog around and then knit 1 rnd. Work one more rnd k2tog around, Cut yarn and pull through rem sts. Weave in tail neatly on WS.

HALF GLOVES

Sizes Women's – Men's
(small – large).
Choose your own colors, use leftovers from jacket or see choices on chart.
With larger dpn, CO 38 (40) sts; join being careful not to twist sts, and work in stockinette for 9 rnds. On next rnd, inc 2 (4) sts evenly spaced around and then knit 1 more rnd. Make picot fold line: *yo, k2tog* or *k2tog, yo*; rep * to * around. See chart for sequence. This allows the points to match the pattern on right and left gloves. Change color and work following chart H (large) and J (small). Right and left gloves are both charted.
Inc for thumb gusset as shown. Place the 9 (11) thumb gusset sts on a holder. CO 9 (11) new sts over the gap. Continue following chart. When the glove reaches base of little finger (about 1 ¼- 1 ½ in / 3-4 cm above thumbhole), cut yarn. Begin again at "note" on chart and continue from this point. Knit 1 rnd leaving 6 sts from front and 6 sts from back to place on holder. CO 1 st between. Knit 1 rnd. Fingers are all worked in the same color. It is easiest if you place the sts for each finger on a separate holder. Each finger is marked on chart.

Index finger: Work with the last 7 (8) sts from back of hand and 6 (7) sts from palm; CO 2 sts between these = 15 (17) sts. Knit 7 (8) rnds or to desired length. BO as for sleeve top finishing (see Techniques).

Middle finger: Work with 7 (8) sts from back of hand and 6 (7) from palm and CO 2 sts between these against next finger. Pick up 1 st from previous CO for a total of 16 (18) sts. Knit 6 (7) rnds and BO.

Ring finger: Work with the last 13 sts of back and palm. Pick up and knit 1 (2) sts from previous CO for a total of 14 (15) sts. Knit 5 (6) rnds and BO.

Little finger: Work with the last 12 sts and pick up and knit 1 st from previous CO. Knit 5 (6) rnds and BO.

Thumb: Move sts from holder to ndl and pick up and knit 9 (11) sts from top of thumbhole. On the large glove, k2tog at each side of the 1st rnd so that there are 20 sts. Knit around for ¾-1 ¼ in / 2-3 cm or to desired length.

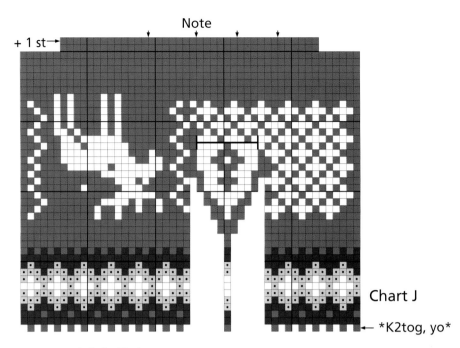

Chart J

← *K2tog, yo*

Women's left half-glove

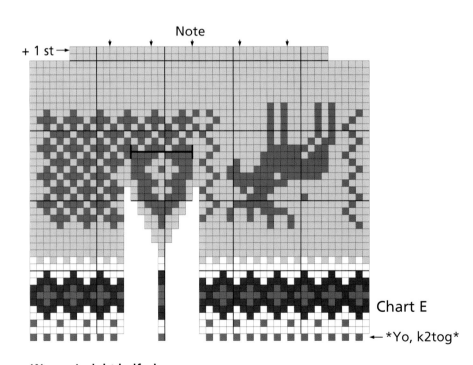

Chart E

← *Yo, k2tog*

Women's right half-glove

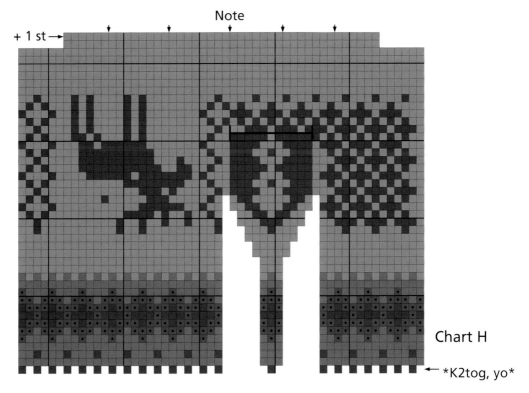

Men's left half-glove

Chart H

← *K2tog, yo*

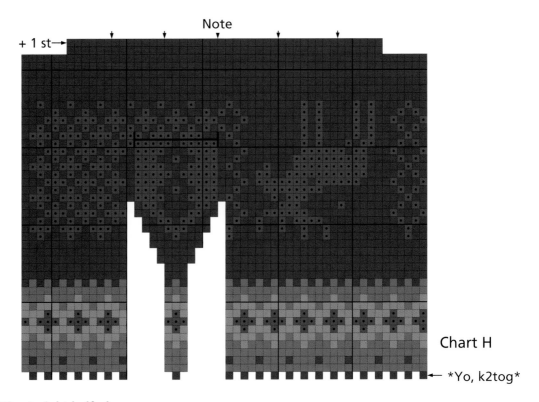

Men's right half-glove

Chart H

← *Yo, k2tog*

Women's Short And Long Jackets

Level of Difficulty: 2-3

Sizes	S	(M)	L	(XL)
Short Jacket				
Chest	42 ½	(45 ¼)	48	(51 ¼) in
	108	(115)	122	(130) cm
Length, approx	19 ¾	(20)	21	(21 ¾) in
	50	(51)	53	(55) cm
Sleeve length, approx	18 ½	(19)	19	(19 ¼) in
	47	(48)	48	(49) cm
Long Jacket				
Chest	44	(47 ¼)	50 ½	(53 ½) in
	112	(120)	128	(136) cm
Length, approx	26 ½	(26 ¾)	27 ¼	(27 ½) in
	67	(68)	69	(70) cm
Sleeve length, approx	18 ½	(19)	19	(19 ¼) in
	47	(48)	48	(49) cm

Yarn: Telemark (100% wool, 153 yds/ 140 m per 50 g (note: Telemark is no longer available)

	MC	CC1	CC2	CC3	CC4
Short Jacket	blue 5946	light blue 5944	gray 2621	old rose 4745	
Long Jacket	white 1012	light gray 1033	gray 1053	black 1099	light blue 5944
Alternate	white 1012	light gray 1033	gray 1053	dark red	red or light rust or rust

Yarn Amounts

Short Jacket

MC	7	7	8	9 balls
CC1	4	5	6	7 balls
CC2	1	1	1	1-2 balls
CC3	1	1	1	1 ball

Long Jacket

MC	6	7	8	9 balls
CC1	9	10	11	12 balls
CC2	1	1	1-2	2 balls
CC3	1	1	1	1 ball
CC4	1	1	1	1 ball

Needles: US size 2 or 4 / 3 or 3.5 mm (make gauge swatch first).

Gauge: 25 sts and about 28-30 rows = 4 x 4 in / 10 x 10 cm. Adjust needle size to obtain correct gauge.

Notions:
Short Jacket: 1 silver clasp from Silverfox NC 1, small.
Long Jacket: 8-10 pewter buttons "Selbu."

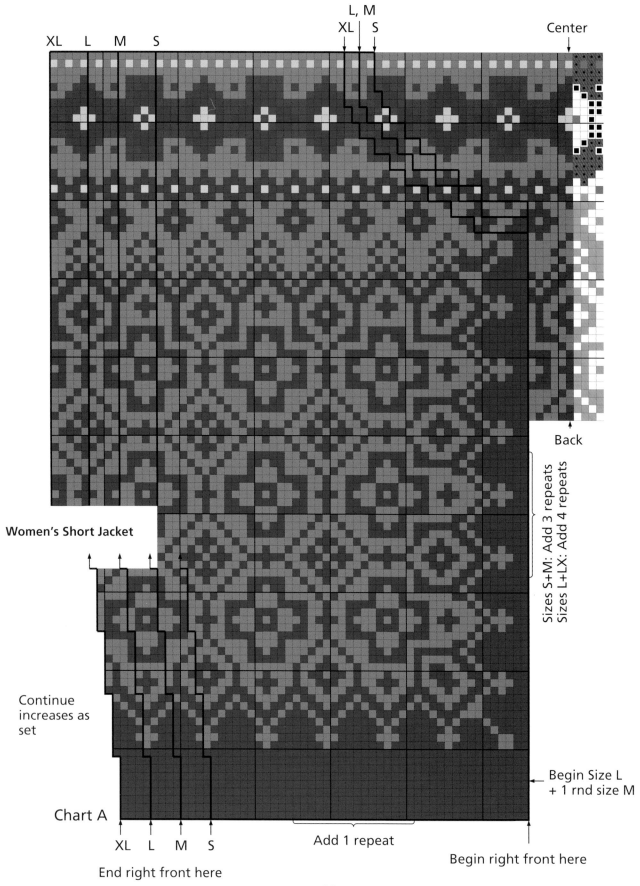

XL   L   M   S

L, M

XL   S

Center

Back

Sizes S+M: Add 3 repeats
Sizes L+LX: Add 4 repeats

Women's Short Jacket

Continue
increases as
set

Begin Size L
+ 1 rnd size M

Chart A

XL   L   M   S

Add 1 repeat

End right front here

Begin right front here

Women's Long Jacket

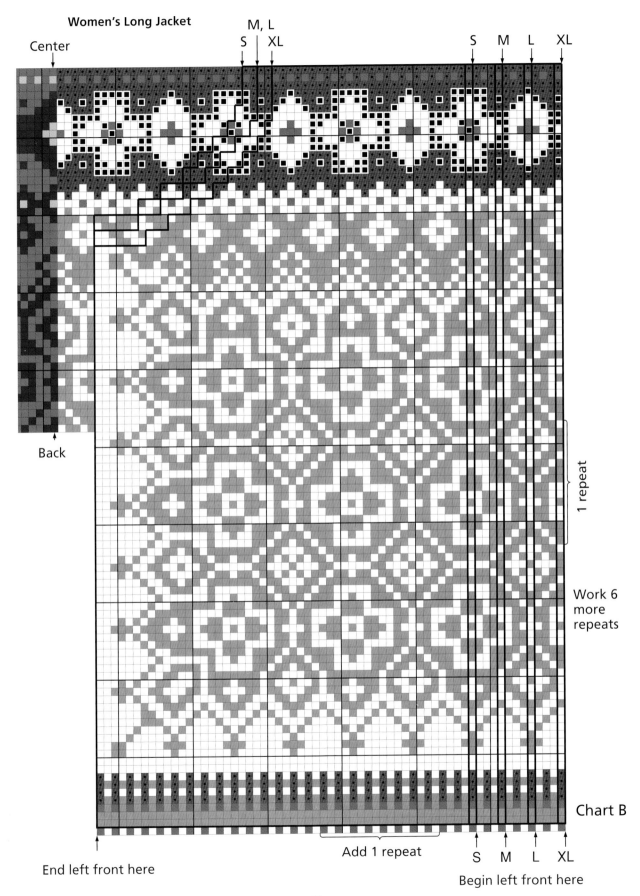

Center

M, L
S XL

S M L XL

Back

1 repeat

Work 6
more
repeats

Chart B

End left front here

Add 1 repeat

S M L XL

Begin left front here

67

WOMEN'S SHORT JACKET
Body

With MC, CO 219 (234) 248 (263) sts and work 10 rows back and forth in stockinette. On the next row, inc 22 (23) 25 (26) sts with m1 after every 10th st = 241 (257) 273 (289) sts. Work 2 more rows in stockinette and then purl 1 row on RS (fold line). *At the same time*, CO 4 sts at end of row for the steek at center front. Steek is worked throughout with k1 CC1, 2 sts with both yarns, k1 with CC1. *Note:* Steek sts are not included in any stitch counts.

Change to circular and join to work in the round. Pm at side sts: K57 (61) 65 (69), pm around next st after knitting it (right side st). K125 (133) 141 (149), pm around next st after knitting it (left side st).
Note: To accommodate the pattern repeats for the total length, you must work 9 (10) 4 (9) rnds with MC before beginning pattern. For this reason, the increases at the sides will not match the chart exactly for sizes M and L.
The chart shows some of the increases on each side of each side st. These increases begin 8 (10) 10 (12) rnds after the fold line. Inc on every 8th rnd for all sizes a total of 7 (8) 8 (9) times.
Although the side sts are marked on charts for front and back, do not repeat them on the back – each side st is worked only once and the pattern reverses from these side sts. Begin at the same arrow for the right front on all sizes. Work 1 repeat extra in width (see chart). MC is used throughout back.
After completing all the increases, each front should have 64 (69) 73 (78) sts and the back 139 (149) 157 (167) sts, not including side sts. One repeat in length (16 rnds) = approx 2 ¼ in / 5.5 cm. Follow the chart and add 3 (3) 4 (4) repeats in length. If you want a longer jacket, lengthen at this point.

The top panel is worked with 3 colors. It can be a bit tricky to work back and forth with 3 colors so we recommend that you work straight up in the round and then machine-stitch and cut the neck opening. See chart and place pins or a marking thread along the decrease line, and then machine-stitch a little inside the marked line with small zigzag sts. Sew an extra seam just inside the first. At center front sew a little back and forth so that the sts won't slide out when you cut open the front.
I prefer to reinforce the steeks as described above but, if that seems too scary, you can try other methods, such as crochet or machine-stitch 2 rows of straight stitches close together. In any case, the last 3 rows should be worked back and forth. BO the 2 side sts and work the last 3 rows.

Shape the neckline and continue working back and forth as shown on chart. Make sure you have the same number of stitches left for each shoulder.
Note: For size M, work 3 extra rows at the end to get the correct length. This might make the neck opening a bit large. Measure the length before beginning neck shaping and begin 3 rows past the one shown on the chart.
If desired, you can add 2-3 rows extra to get to the right length. Shoulder finishing: join with three-needle bind-off as explained in Techniques.

Finishing body

All of the bands are worked with MC. Machine-stitch and cut front. With RS facing, pick up and knit 4 and then 3-4 sts for every 4 rows along one side of front. Decide if you want a garter ridge along the band. Work 6 rows in stockinette back and forth and then purl 1 row on RS for fold line and make a fac-

ing the same width as band. Work other side of front the same way. Neckband is worked in one color. With RS facing, pick up and knit sts around neck. Knit back (1 ridge, if desired). Work a total of 6 rows stockinette back and forth, but, on the 5th row, dec 6 sts evenly spaced across row. Purl 1 row on RS for fold line and then work facing same width as neckband. On the 3rd row, inc 6 sts at same places where you had previously decreased. BO loosely and sew down all facings on WS.

Sleeves

With CC1, CO 61 (65) 69 (75) sts; join, being careful not to twist cast-on row. Knit in stockinette for facing and, at the same time, dec 1 st on each side of the 2 center sts at underarm on every 4th rnd 3 times to 55 (59) 63 (69) sts. When sleeve measures approx 2 in / 5 cm, purl 1 row on RS (fold line).
Work sleeve following chart C, beginning at arrow for your size. Inc on each side of the 2 underarm sts on every 4th rnd. You should work 2 more repeats in length than shown on chart.
Continue following chart and then measure sleeve after working charted rows. You might need to knit a few extra rounds in one color.
Note: Size S ends with 1 extra rnd in one color (see chart).
Purl 6 rows on RS for facing. BO loosely with sleeve top finishing (see Techniques). Measure top of sleeve; half the width = armhole depth. Measure depth of armhole down from shoulder seam and then machine-stitch and cut armholes. Attach sleeve from RS; sew down facings.

WOMEN'S LONG JACKET
Body

With CC1, CO 254 (269) 283 (298) sts and work 10 rows in stockinette back and forth. On the next row, inc with m1 after about every 11th st 23 (24) 26 (27) sts to 277 (293) 309 (325) sts. Work 2 more rows and then join to knit in the round. Leaving CC1 hanging, join CC4 (old rose) and work picot fold line: *k2tog, yo*; rep * to * around, end k1. *At the same time*, CO 4 sts at end of row for center front steek. Work steek sts throughout as: k1 with CC1, 2 sts with both yarns, k1 with CC2. *Note:* Steek sts are not included in any stitch counts.

Now work following chart B. Begin at the same arrow for right front for all sizes. Add 1 rep in width (see chart).

The first two rnds are single color. In addition, work 0 (0) 2 (2) rnds with the same color before beginning pattern.

Work the first panel following chart and then knit 2 rnds with MC and then work 0 (2) 2 (4) rnds with the same color. Continue following chart and pm at side sts. Knit 66 (70) 74 (78) sts, pm around next st after knitting it (right side). Knit across back 143 (151) 159 (167) sts, pm around next st after knitting it (left side). The pattern reverses at the side sts.

Continue charted rows. Add 2 repeats in width for both front and back. Work 6 extra repeats in length. Each repeat measures approx 2 ¼ in / 5.5 cm. Lengthen or shorten jacket here.

The top panel is worked with 3 colors. See explanation under Short Jacket for neck shaping. The last 3 rows should be worked back and forth.

After completing, work 0 (1) 1 (1) row. Shoulder finishing: see three-needle bind-off in Techniques.

Finishing Body

If you have knitted straight up, see instructions for short Jacket. Machine-stitch and cut center front.

For each front band, with CC1, pick up and knit 4 or 3-4 sts for every 4 rows and knit back.

The button band is a single color. Decide whether you want buttons or clasps.

For clasps: Work about 7 rows back and forth and then purl 1 row on RS for fold line. Work facing as wide as band and then BO loosely. For this style, the front bands abut rather than overlap.

For buttons: Pick up and knit sts as explained above and then knit back. On the left front band, work 9 rows stockinette, purl 1 row on RS for fold line and then work facing same width.

On the right front band, make buttonholes. Work 3 rows after ridge. On the next row, BO for buttonholes. Decide how many buttons

Women's Sleeve

L+XL

M

S
(+ 1 single-color row)

+ 2 repeats

1 repeat

Chart C

Center st

S | L XL
M

you want; the top one is 2 sts from the edge. Mark spacing: each buttonhole is worked over 4 sts for larger or 3 sts for smaller buttons. On the model, the buttonholes are placed so that they match pattern repeats and a difference of 1 st between holes doesn't matter. On next row CO the same number of sts as bound off over gaps and continue until you've worked a total of 9 rows stockinette; purl 1 row on RS for fold line and then make facing, spacing buttonholes to match band. See section on buttonholes in Techniques.

Split yarn and sew hem stitch around each buttonhole to make each secure and neat. Make sure bound-off sts are not visible and that the holes are not pulled in too much. Sew down facings.

Neckband
Pick up and knit sts around neck from ridge at button band; make sure you have an odd number of sts for chart G = multiple of 2+1. Knit back = 1 ridge. Work neckband following chart G + 2 rows. Change to MC and make picot fold line: K1, *k2tog, yo*; rep * to *. Make facing same width as band. BO and then sew down facing on WS.

Sleeves with Stockinette Cuffs
Follow instructions for short jacket sleeves. Work the first panel following chart D and then continue with chart C.

Sleeves with Ribbed Cuffs
With CC3, CO 48 (50) 52 (52) sts, join. Work in stockinette for approx 4 rnds. Turn work so that WS faces out. Change to CC2. Knit 1 rnd and then work in k1tbl, p1 ribbing for 1 ½-2 in / 4-5 cm. On the next rnd, inc 15 (17) 19 (25) sts evenly spaced around to 63 (67) 71 (77) sts. Now work following chart D, the 3 first rnds after "note," and then

follow chart C. Increase as shown on chart and follow instructions for Short Jacket sleeves.

Long Jacket, Sleeve Cuff

Note →

Fold line →

Chart D

Long Jacket, Neckband

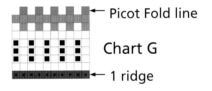

← Picot Fold line

Chart G

← 1 ridge

Man's Jacket

Level of Difficulty: 2

Sizes	M	(L)	XL	XXL
Chest	47 ¼ in/120 cm	50 ½ in/128 cm	53 ½ in/136 cm	56 ¾ in/144 cm
Length	about 25 ¼ in/64 cm	25 ½ in/65 cm	27 ½ in/70 cm	30 in/76 cm
Sleeve length	19 ¼ in/49 cm	19 ¾ in/50cm	20 in/51 cm	20 ½ in/52 cm

Yarn: Telemark (100% wool, 153 yds / 140 m per 50 g
(note: Telemark is no longer available)
Main Color (MC) Contrast Color (CC)
Charcoal 1088 Gray 1053 (CC)

Yarn amounts:

MC	8-9	9	10	11 balls
CC	6-7	7	8	9 balls

Needles: US size 3 or 4 / 3 or 3.5 mm (make a gauge swatch first) —32 in / 80 cm circular for body and shorter circular + set of dpn for sleeves.

Gauge: 25 sts and 28-30 rows = 4 x 4 in / 10 x 10 cm. Adjust needle size to obtain correct gauge.

Notions: 8-10 pewter buttons "Bachelors."

MAN'S JACKET
Body
With MC, CO 269 (283) 298 (313) sts. Work back and forth in stockinette for 10 rows (the first row = WS). On the next row, increase 24 (26) 27 (28) sts with m1 after about every 11th st = 293 (309) 325 (341) sts. Work 2 more rows in stockinette and then purl 1 row on RS. Now join to work in the round. CO 4 extra sts at the end of the round. These sts form the "steek" which will be cut open later for center front. Always work them as: 1 st CC, 2 sts with both yarns, 1 st CC. *Note:* Steek sts are not included in any stitch counts.

Begin with 2 (5) 2 (2) rnds MC. On the last rnd, place markers: Knit 70 (74) 78 (82) sts, place marker around next st after knitting it (right side). Knit 151 (159) 167 (175) sts for back, place marker around next st after knitting it (left side). Begin pattern. The arrows on the chart indicate side sts. Don't forget to work 2 extra pattern repeats across both fronts and the back. Continue, following the chart and working 6 (6) 7 (8) pattern repeats in length after the initial repeat. Each repeat measures 2 ¼ in / 5.5 cm. If you wish to length or shorten

the jacket, do so before completing pattern. After completing pattern, shape neck. BO the 2 side sts, work back and forth and bind off as shown on chart.
Shoulders: join with three-needle bind-off (see Techniques).

Sleeves
Chart F
With CC and dpn, CO 59 (65) 65 (71) sts. Work in stockinette for 9 (11) 13 (15) rnds and then purl 1 rnd on RS. On the next rnd, inc 6 sts evenly spaced around (inc with k1f&b). Work sleeve following chart F. Begin at the arrow for chosen size.

Note: On size M, work 1 rnd with CC before beginning charted pattern.

Inc on each side of the 2 sts centered at underarm on every 4th rnd; work 4 more repeats in length where repeat is marked on chart. Continue, following the chart. When sleeve is complete, measure it. If necessary, work a few more rnds with MC. If there are a number of rnds to work for desired sleeve length, add "lice" to the plain rows. Finish with 6 rnds purl on RS for facing. Bind off loosely as explained in Techniques.

Finishing—Body

Machine-stitch and cut up center of steek.

All of the edgings are worked with MC only.

If using hook or clasp closures, see explanation for women's Long Jacket but make the bands a bit wider; for example, knit 9 rows and then purl 1 row on RS plus 9 rows stockinette for facing. If you want buttonholes, see explanation for women's Long Jacket, but bind off for buttonholes on 5th row. Buttonholes should be on the left side. For each buttonhole, bind off 4 sts. There should also be a button at the top on the neckband. The top buttonhole should be about 3-4 sts from top. On the model the buttonholes are placed so that they flow into the pattern. To fit the buttons within the design, you can work 1 st more or less between buttonholes.

Neckband: Work 2 rows narrower than front bands. With MC, pick up and knit sts around the neck and knit back = 1 ridge. Work 3 rows in stockinette. On the next row, bind off 4 sts for buttonhole at front, beginning about 4 sts inside the edge. On the 5th row, k2tog at 2 places along the curves of each front and at 1 place at each curve on the back, as well at each shoulder seam(= 8 sts dec). CO 4 new sts over buttonhole gap. Continue until there are a total of 9 rows. On the next row, k2tog at 4 places around neck. Purl 1 row on RS (fold line). Continue in stockinette for facing. On the 5th row of facing, increase 8 sts, spaced as for previous decreases. Don't forget the buttonhole on rows 4 and 5. BO loosely. Sew down all facings on WS.

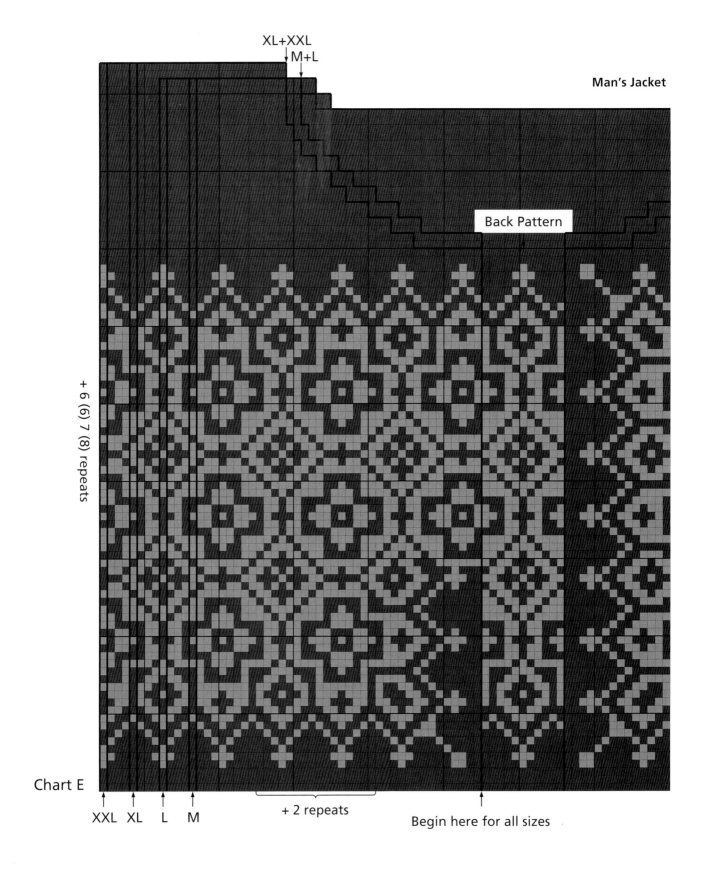

XL+XXL

M+L

Man's Jacket

Back Pattern

+ 6 (6) 7 (8) repeats

Chart E

XXL XL L M

+ 2 repeats

Begin here for all sizes

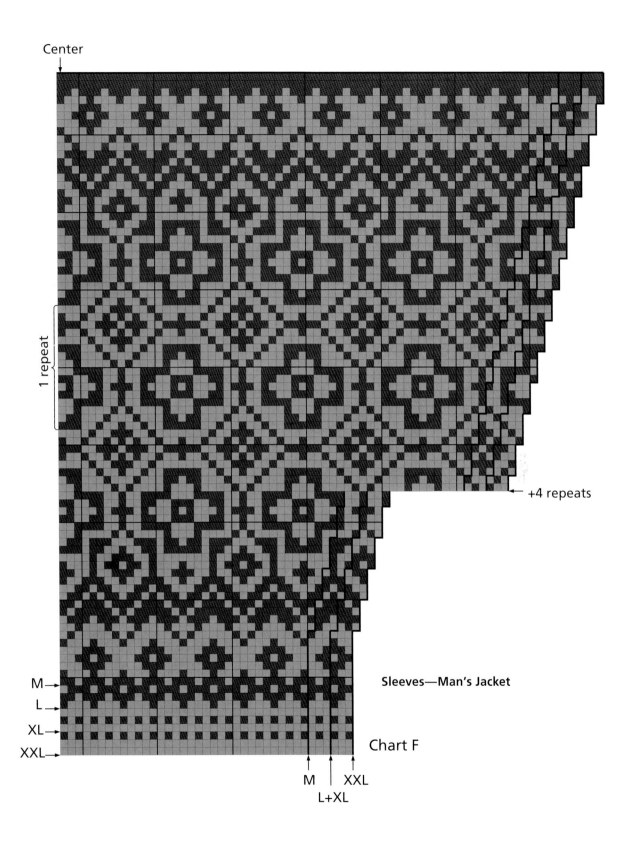

Center

1 repeat

+4 repeats

M →
L →
XL →
XXL →

Sleeves—Man's Jacket

Chart F

M | XXL
L+XL

Cozy Jacket and Vest

Women's
Jacket, vest, cap, wrist warmers

Level of Difficulty: Jacket 2, Vest 2-3

Jacket

Sizes	S	(M)	L
Chest	46 in / 117 cm	(48 in / 122 cm)	50 in / 127 cm
Length	26 ½ in / 67 cm	(27 ½ in / 70 cm)	28 ¾ in / 73 cm
Sleeve length	17 ¼ in / 44 cm	(17 ¾ in / 45 cm)	18 ¼ in / 46 cm

Vest

Width	38 ¼ in / 97 cm	(40 ¼ in / 102 cm)	41 ¾ in / 106 cm

Yarn: Smart (100% superwash wool, 110 yds / 100 m per 50 g)

Jacket	MC	CC1	CC2
	dark green 9084	rust red 4038	light green 9544
OR	cola 1088	rust red 4038	gray 1053

Vest			
	yellow 2417	orange 3619	rust red 4038
OR	white 101	light gray 1042	yellow 2417

Yarn Amounts

Jacket:

MC	13	14	15 balls
CC1	1	1	1-2 balls
CC2	1	1	1 ball

Vest:

MC	3	4	4 balls
CC1	3	3	3-4 balls
CC2	1	1	1 ball

Cap (1 size):

MC	2 balls
CC1	1 ball
CC2	1 ball or leftover yarn from jacket

Needles: US size 4 / 3.5 mm. Long and short circulars + dpn. One size smaller dpn and crochet hook for wrist warmers.

Gauge: 24 sts and approx 30 rows = 4 in / 10 cm. Adjust needle size to obtain correct gauge.

Notions: 9-11 Pewter buttons "Aase."

Wrist Warmers (1 size): leftover yarn from jacket or 1 ball of each color. The wrist warmers weigh about 2.5 oz / 70 gr.

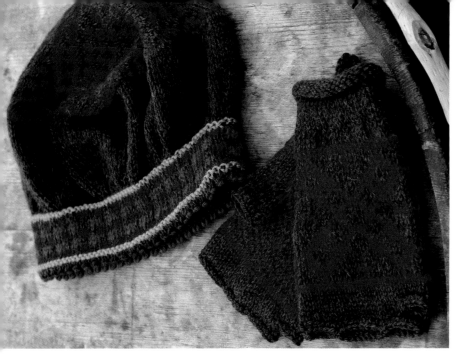

JACKET
Body
With MC, CO 258 (270) 283 sts, join, being careful not to twist cast-on row. Knit 18 rounds in stockinette for facing. Make picot fold line: *k2tog, yo*; rep * to * around (end with k1 on size Large). Knit 2 rnds after fold line, increasing 21 (23) 24 sts evenly spaced around with m1 after about every 12th st = 279 (293) 307 sts. Knit 1 rnd and then work chart ABA (a multiple of 7+2); do not work patterning over last 4 sts of rnd = steek.

Note: The last 4 sts of the round are the steek sts and should be knitted with both yarns on pattern rows. Cut CC and continue only in MC. Pm at 1 st at each side = 68 (72) 75 sts for each front and 137 (143) 151 sts on the back + the 2 side sts and the 4 front steek sts.

When body measures approx 17 (18 ¼) 19 in / 43 (46) 48 cm or desired length to underarm, BO 13 (15) 15 sts centered at each underarm. On the next rnd, CO 4 new sts (steek) over each gap so you can continue to work in the round.

Shape armhole on each side of steek sts:

On fronts: dec 1 st on every rnd 6 times and then on every other rnd 3 times.

On each side of back: dec 1 st on every rnd 4 (2) 1 times and on every other rnd 7 (9) 10 times = 221 (231) 245 sts rem (including all) steek sts. Work until armholes are approx 5 ½ (6 ¼) 6 ¾ in /14 (16) 17 cm from last dec and then shape neckline. BO the center front 24 (26) 28 sts and work back and forth on each section separately. At neck edge on each front, on every other row, BO 3-2-2-1-1-1 (3-2-2-1-1-1) 3-2-1-1-1-1 sts. Place each set of front shoulder sts on holders and work back neck until it is same length as front. BO the center 35 (37) 39 sts on back. There should now be 35 (37) 40 sts for each shoulder. Join shoulders with three-needle bind-off (see Techniques).

Sleeves
With CC1, CO 50 (52) 54 sts, join, and knit 22 rnds for facing. On the next rnd, inc evenly spaced around to 55 (57) 59 sts. Make picot fold line: *k2tog, yo*; rep * to * around and end k1. Change to MC and work chart C (note that fold line is included on chart). Work the extra sts between arrows for your size in color/pattern as for first and last sts of chart. For ridges, knit 1 rnd, purl

1 rnd. After the last ridge, knit 1 rnd with MC. On the next rnd, inc evenly spaced around to 71 (77) 83 sts. Cut CC and continue with MC only. On every 4th rnd, inc on each side of the 2 center underarm sts to 117 (123) 129 sts. Work even until sleeve measures 17 ¼ (17 ¾) 18 ½ in / 44 (45) 47 cm. BO 13 (15) 15 sts centered at underarm and then begin working back and forth. At each side, BO 3 sts 4 (5) 6 times 2 sts 10 times and 3 sts 5 (4) 3 times. BO rem sts.

Neckband
With CC2, pick up and knit 100-107 sts around neck – you'll need a multiple of 7+2. Knit back for a ridge. Work 1 row with MC, beginning with a purl row and then purl back so that pattern begins on a RS row. Work charts B and A, beginning at arrow.

Work 2 rows in stockinette, a picot fold line and then about 10 rows for facing. BO loosely. Sew down neckband facing with split yarn.

Button bands
Machine-stitch and cut front opening. Work each band separately. With CC2, pick up and knit sts on each side of front: pick up 3-4 sts, skip 1. Make sure you have an odd number of sts so you can begin and end band with same color for chart D. Knit back for a ridge. Work chart D and then in stockinette with MC. Make buttonholes on one side of front: work 2 rows following chart D. Mark spacing for buttonholes. The top one is about ⅝ in / 1 ½ cm below neckband and the bottom one about ¾ in / 2 cm from lower edge. Decide how many sts to BO for each buttonhole (2 or 3 sts) and how many buttons to use (8-9) and space holes accordingly. BO for each buttonhole and CO the same number of sts over each gap on following row. Work 3 more rows and purl 1 row on RS for fold line. Make

facing same width as band, spacing buttonholes as for band. Sew down button bands and then sew around each buttonhole (see Techniques). Make other band the same way, without buttonholes. Sew on buttons and sew down facings on WS. Instead of making a buttonhole on the patterned neckband, sew a button loop (see Techniques) and attach button to other side. Attach a decorative button below it.

Attaching Sleeves

Measure top of sleeve; half the width = armhole depth. Measure depth of armhole down from shoulder seam and then machine-stitch and cut armholes. With CC2, pick up and knit sts around each sleeve top. Working back and forth, purl 1 row on RS and then work facing in reverse stockinette with MC: knit 1 row on RS and then purl 5 rows on RS. Attach sleeves with RS facing so that the pattern color ridge shows. Sew down facing on WS.

VEST

This vest is designed as a short cropped vest. If you want a longer vest, you will need to make some adjustments. Take precise measurements and try on the vest in progress. You could add an extra repeat at the stomach or at armholes.

Chart E shows one front and half of the back. Sizes are marked with arrows and dark lines. The side sts are indicated on both sides of front for size L and on only one side for the other sizes. Color in the side stitches for your size.

Work the side sts as follows: Add a CC strand for each stripe. Work to the black line on chart, add the two other strands to the left, work the stripe (1 st), move this strand to the left, bring the two other strands around and follow the chart.

With CC1, CO 198 (210) 222 sts; join, being careful not to twist cast-on row. Knit in stockinette for 22 rnds for facing. On the next-to-last rnd, inc 14 sts evenly spaced around = 212 (224) 236 sts. Make picot fold line: *k2tog, yo*; rep * to * around. Now knit chart D, beginning at arrow for your size.

Note: On size S, omit 1 rep in length as noted on chart.

Inc on each side of side st on every 10th row following chart to a total of 232 (252) 264 sts. Work to desired length to underarm. If you want to add an extra repeat, you should do so at the place marked for omitted rep for size S. Shape armholes as shown on chart: 21 (23) 23 sts dec. On the next rnd, CO 3 new sts for steek over each armhole. Shape front and back of

Lower edge of body

A
B
A

Beg and end here for all sizes

Button bands

 D

Note that charts offer color variations, not intarsia knit in multi-colors.

Sleeve panel

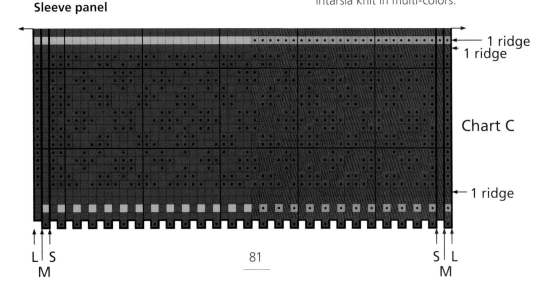

1 ridge
1 ridge

Chart C

1 ridge

L S   S L
M   M

Center
back

Vest

Chart D

S M L   L M S

82

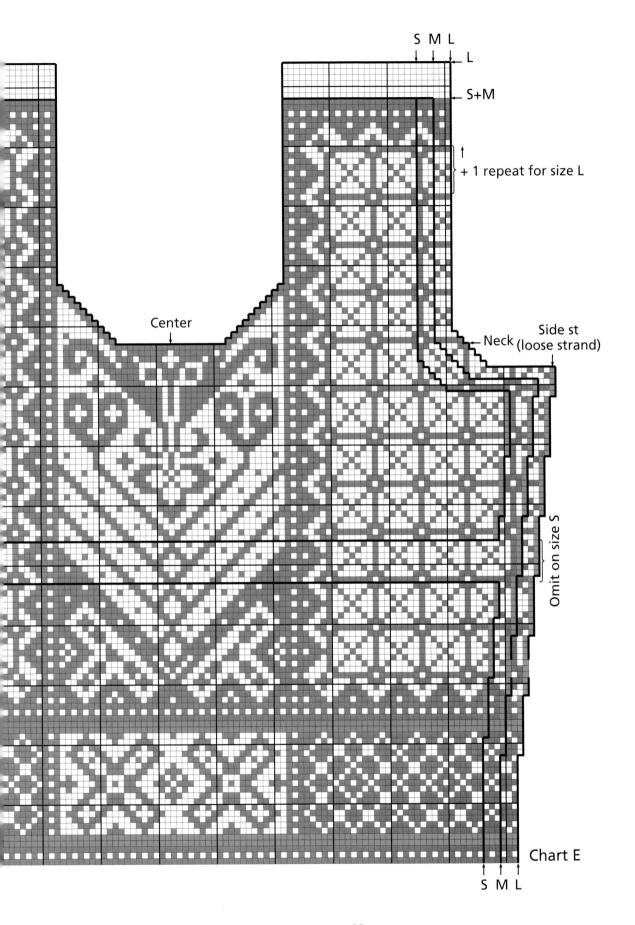

S M L

L

S+M

+ 1 repeat for size L

Center

Neck

Side st
(loose strand)

Omit on size S

Chart E

S M L

armhole on every rnd as shown on chart 5 (6) 6 times.

When front is complete, shape neckline: BO 19 sts at center front. CO 3 new sts as steek over gap and then shape back and front neck as

shown on chart. Complete charted rows for your size or to desired length. At back neck, BO 33 sts, and BO the center steek sts at front and armholes. For the rest of the vest, each part is worked separately back and forth. Work the very last row with CC2 (not shown on chart). Join shoulders with three-needle bind-off using CC2 (see Techniques).

Finishing

Machine-stitch and cut front neck and armholes at each side.
Sew down facings with split yarn.
Neckband: With CC2, pick up and knit sts around neck. On the front and back, pick up 1 st in each st and on the sides, pick up 3-4 sts, skip 1; join.
Knit 5 rnds in stockinette and dec 2 sts at each side of the 2 sts at each corner on rnds 1 and 3. K2tog tbl or ssk before corner and k2tog after corner. At center back, dec 2 sts on the 3rd rnd the same way. Now purl 1 rnd for fold line and then

knit 4 rnds in stockinette for facing, increasing on rnds 2 and 4 where you had previously decreased. BO loosely. Fold facing to WS and sew down loosely with split yarn.

Armhole bands: Pick up and knit sts around the armhole as for neckband. Knit 5 rnds stockinette, with k2tog on rnds 1 and 3 at each curve at bottom of armhole as well as centered at underarm (= 3 sts dec on rnd). Work fold line and facing as for neckband, increasing on rnds 2 and 4 where you had decreased on band.
BO loosely and sew down facings on WS with split yarn.

CAP

Chart F shows the crown of the cap and G shows the brim pattern.
With CC1, CO 27 sts. Work back and forth in stockinette following chart F. The first row of the chart = cast-on row. Inc at beg and end of every row: at beg of row, CO 1 new st; at end, k1f&b into last st. Work outermost st at either beginning or end of row with both strands of yarn. The pattern will look neater when the yarn goes all the way out to the edge and these stitches will be hidden once the stitches are picked up for the brim. When decreasing for the crown, BO first st and k2tog at end of row. On last row of chart, BO all sts across.
With the same color as for last row of crown, pick up and knit sts around the crown: 27 sts along each of the straight sides and 28 sts along each diagonal line = 220 sts. Join.
Knit 18 rnds in stockinette. On the next rnd, dec: *k2tog, k2*; rep * to * around = 165 sts.
Knit 2 rnds. On next rnd, dec: *k2tog, k1*; rep * to * around = 110 sts. Knit 1 rnd, dec 2 more sts and then work following chart G, beginning with a ridge in CC2 (see Jacket). Next work the panel with

Jacket's CC1 for and vest's CC1. After the final ridge, knit 1 rnd with MC (Jacket color). Change to vest's CC1 and make picot edge: *k2tog, yo*; rep * to * around. Change back to jacket color and knit facing to same width as brim pattern. Work tightly or knit with smaller needles.
Sew down facing with split yarn.

WRIST WARMERS

Chart H shows the left mitt; the right is worked in reverse image. With larger needles (set of 5 dpn), CO 36 sts, divide sts onto 4 ndls, and join to work in the round. Change to smaller needles and knit 14 rnds in stockinette (edge rolls up). On the next rnd, inc 8 sts, evenly spaced around. Knit 1 more rnd and then work following chart H. Change to larger ndls when pattern motif begins. Inc for thumb as shown on chart with m1 inside the edge st on both sides of the thumb gusset. When there are 9 sts for thumb gusset, knit across them with waste yarn; slide sts back to left needle and knit again with pattern yarn. Continue, following the chart. After finishing pattern, change to smaller needles. Knit to desired length up little finger. On the next rnd, BO the last 5 sts on the 2nd needle and the first 5 sts on the 3rd ndl = 10 sts for little finger. On the next rnd, CO 2 new sts over the gap. Knit another 2 rnds and then BO.
Remove waste yarn and pick up 9 sts from front and 10 sts from back. Knit 2 rnds and then k2tog at beg of the next rnd = 18 sts rem. Knit 4 rnds and then work 2 rnds in k1/p1 ribbing. BO in ribbing. Single crochet around the top of mitt and between the fingers to close each space.
Steam press carefully on all but the rolled wrist.

Cap Crown

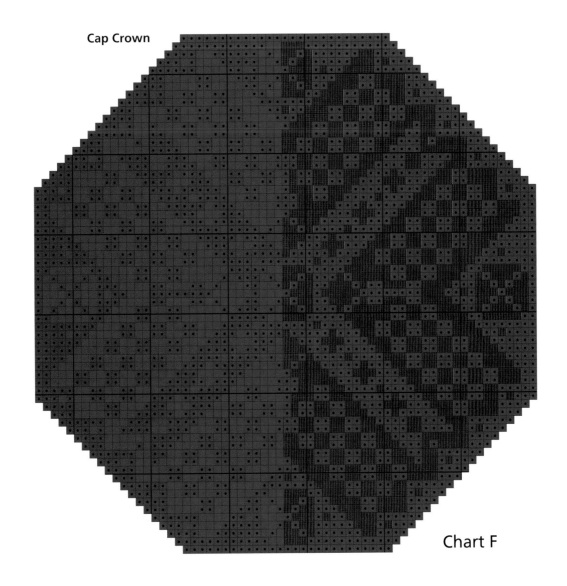

Chart F

Cap Brim panel

Chart G

← 1 ridge

← 1 ridge

Beg and
end here

Note: The charts show color alternatives and are
not for intarsia knitting (see Charts in Techniques)

Wrist Warmers

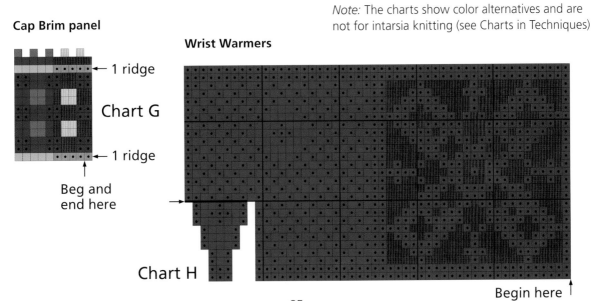

Chart H

Begin here ↑

Ribbed Sweater and Vest

Women's
Ribbed Sweater
Vest

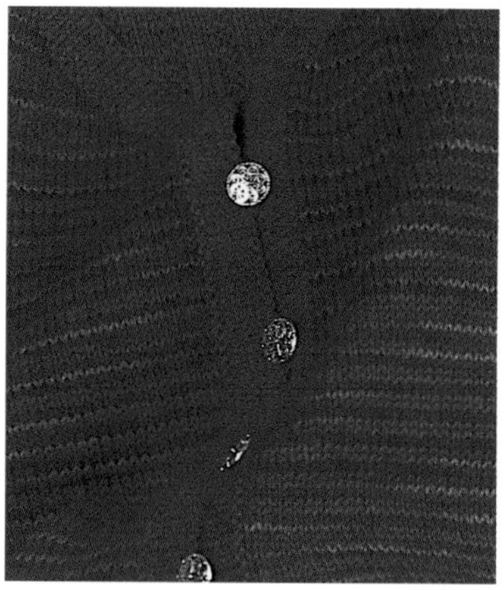

Level of Difficulty: 2

Sweater

Sizes	S	(M)	L
Chest	36 ¼ in / 92 cm	(37 ¾ in / 96 cm)	39 ½ in / 100 cm
Length	23 ¾ in / 60 cm	(24 ½ in / 62 cm)	25 ½ in / 64 cm
Sleeve length	16 ½ in / 42 cm	(17 ¼ in / 44 cm)	18 ¼ in / 46 cm

Vest

Sizes	S	(M)	L
Chest	40 ¼ in / 102 cm	(43 in / 109 cm)	45 ¾ in / 116 cm
Length	20 ½ in / 52 cm	(21 ¼ in / 54 cm)	22 in / 56 cm

Yarn: Smart (100% superwash wool, 110 yds / 100 m per 50 g)
Sweater: red 4038 or dark blue 5575.
Vest: flame red 4027 and red 4038 or flame blue 6350 and blue 5575

Yarn Amounts

Sweater	11	12	13 balls

Vest			
MC	6	6	7 balls
CC for edging	4	5	5-6 balls

Needles: US size 2 or 4 / 3 or 3.5 mm—long and short circulars + dpn.

Gauge: 24 sts and approx 29 rows = 4 in / 10 cm. Adjust needle size to obtain correct gauge.

Notions: 16-20 buttons for the sides and front of vest. For our model, we used 26 pewter buttons "Sissel," 20 buttons for the sides and 6 for the front.

SWEATER
Body
CO 220 (230) 240 sts; join, being careful not to twist cast-on row. (Knit 1 rnd and then work 1 rnd in p2, k3 ribbing) 4 times. Begin with p1, k3 and end rnd with p1.
Work lace rnd: *K2tog, k1, k2tog tbl, yo twice (wrap yarn twice around needle)*; rep * to * around. Knit 1 rnd, working k1, p1 into each double yarnover.

Begin stripe pattern: Rnd 1: K3, p2 around; Rnd 2: Knit.
Work in pattern until piece measures 15 ½ (16 ¼) 17 in / 39 (41) 43 cm. Divide piece at each side, between 2 purl sts, with 110 (115) 120 sts for each section (= k3, p1, pm, work in pattern for 110 sts, pm, complete rnd, including the sts before first marker; beg of row has shifted). Rows now begin and end with p1.

Back
Shape armholes: BO 8 sts at each side, then 3 sts 3 times and 1 st 2 times at each side = 72 (77) 82 sts rem. Work back and forth in pattern until piece measures total length = 23 ¾ (24 ½) 25 ½in / 60 (62) 64 cm.
Shape shoulders with short rows: work until 5 sts rem; turn, sl first st and tighten yarn slightly. Work across until 5 sts rem; turn, sl 1. On

next 2 short rows, work until 10 sts rem at each side, and then work 2 rows until 15 sts rem. On the last row, BO the center 34 (35) 36 sts = 19 (21) 23 sts rem for each shoulder. Place shoulder sts on a holder.

Front

Shape armholes as for back and work until front measures 21 ¾ (22 ½) 23 ¼ in / 55 (57) 59 cm.

Neck shaping: BO the center 24 (25) 26 sts and work each side separately. At neck edge, BO 1 st on every other row 5 (5) 5 times. Continue without shaping until front measures 23 ¾ (24 ½) 25 ½ in / 60 (62) 64 cm.

Shape shoulders as for back, with short rows to the 3 (8) 13 outermost sts at each side = 19 (21) 23 sts rem for each shoulder. Join shoulders with three-needle bind-off (see Techniques).

Neckband

Pick up and knit sts around neck. At front and back, the sts should look as if they continue from body pattern. On the diagonal sides, it is important to pick up a number of sts equal to a multiple of 5, the pattern rep. If there are a few too many, you can k2tog here and there on the first rnd. The neckband should not be too tight. Our size S model has 100 sts around neck.

Join and knit around in pattern for ¾ in / 2 cm for a narrow band or 1 ¼-3 ¼ in / 3-8 cm for a wider band. Make a lace rnd as for body and continue as for band before lace rnd on lower edge of body: Knit 1 rnd, working k1, p1 into each double yarnover and then work 4 repeats of p2/k3 ribbing rnd alternating with knit rnd. BO as for sleeve top finishing (see Techniques).

Sleeves

CO 45 (50) 50 sts, join, and work in ribbing as for body. So that the

last lace hole will be correct, begin with k3, p2. Make the lace rnd as described for body. Continue in pattern stripe. *At the same time*, on every 4th rnd, inc on each side of 2 purl sts at center of underarm until there are 79 (84) 88 sts and sleeve measures 16 ½ (17 ¼) 18 ¼ in / 42 (44) 46 cm (or desired length to armhole). BO 10 sts centered at underarm, begin working back and forth, and then BO 2 sts at beg of every row 4 times, and 1 st at beg of every row 16 (16) 18 times. BO 2 more sts at beg of every row 12 (14) 16 times and 3 sts 2 times. BO rem 15 (16) 14 sts.

Attach sleeves from WS with split yarn. The armholes are wider than the sleeves. Attach sleeves well at underarm and stretch them a bit around rounded edges; the top part should be smooth. Pin baste seam first and check seam from RS to make sure that the decrease lines do not show on the front.

VEST

The vest is worked in 3 sections – 1 main piece and 2 side pieces (under the armholes). Knit the main piece on a circular needle with steeks at each underarm and the center front. Steek sts are included in the stitch counts.

With solid color yarn, CO 165 (178) 191 sts; join. Knit in stockinette for 1 ¼ in / 3 cm for facing. On the next rnd, inc 15 (16) 17 sts, with m1 after about every 11th st = 180 (194) 208 sts. Knit 2 rnds and then purl 1 rnd on RS for fold line. Knit 6 rnds and then purl 1 rnd on RS again. Change to flame/tweed yarn and knit without shaping until piece measures 15 ¾ (16 ¼) 16 ½ in / 40 (41) 42 cm from fold line.

Pm around steek sts; they are no longer included in stitch counts. Knit 41 (44) 47, mark next 4 sts for armhole steek. K86 (94) 102 (= back), pm around next 4 sts for

armhole steek, k41 (44) 47 for other front, pm – last 4 sts are center front steek. Dec 1 st at each side of front steek on every rnd a total of 21 (22) 23 times. SSk at beg of rnd and k2tog at end before steek sts. Each front should now have 20 (22) 24 sts. Continue without shaping until piece measures 19 ¾ (20 ½) 21 ¼ in / 50 (52) 54 cm from fold line. BO the center 2 steek sts at each armhole as well as 30 (32) 34 sts at center back. Now work back and forth. Work front without shaping for ¾ in / 2 cm. On the back BO 4-3-1 (4-3-2) 5-3-2 sts on each side of neck at beg of every row. The shoulders are shaped with short rows (see below). There should be 20 (22) 24 sts for each back shoulder while the front still has 44 (48) 52 sts total.

Back

Shape shoulders with short rows: work until 5 sts remain on outside of shoulder; turn, sl 1 and tighten yarn slightly, work back. Work until 10 sts rem; turn, sl 1, work back. Work until 15 sts rem; turn, sl 1; work back. Change to edge color and work 1 row across all sts and then purl 1 row on RS (work purl row somewhat tightly). Place sts on a holder. Shape other shoulder the same way.

Front: Shape as for back with short rows on both sides. Leave 3 sts at each side, then 8 sts and finally 13 sts. BO the 4 steek sts.

Join shoulders with three-needle bind-off (see Techniques).

Option 1: Side pieces worked back and forth: With solid color yarn, CO 35 (37) 39 sts. Work in stockinette for 1 ¼ in / 3 cm for facing. Knit the facing tighter than for body of the piece. Purl 1 row on RS for fold line and then work 6 rows in stockinette and 1 purl row on RS.

Now work in block pattern with solid color and flame yarn. Each block is 3 sts wide and 4 rows high. You can work the blocks all in stockinette or, as for our models, alternate 1 stockinette block with 1 reverse stockinette one. Work the solid color blocks in stockinette and the flame yarn blocks with knit 1 row, and then reverse stockinette for 3 rows.

Rows 1 and 3: Knit across as follows: Sl 1, k 0 (1) 2 with solid color yarn, alternate k3 with flame yarn, k3 with solid color across, and end with k3 flame, k1 (2) 3 with solid color yarn, working the final st with both strands.

Rows 2 and 4 (WS): Sl 1, p 0 (1) 2 with solid color, alternate k3 with flame, k3 with solid across, and end with k3 flame, p1 (2) 3 working last st with both colors.

Note: Slip the first st on each row and work last st with both yarns. Work in pattern as set until each piece measures 10 ¼ (10 ¾) 11 in / 26 (27) 28 cm from fold line. The final block should be complete. With solid color yarn, knit 1 row and then purl 1 row on RS. Work 7 rows in stockinette and then fold line (purl 1 row on RS) and stockinette for 1 ¼ in / 3 cm for facing; BO.

Option 2: Side pieces worked in the round: Knit both pieces at the same time. CO 78 (84) 90 sts and join. Knit facing as explained above. Work blocks around, with the flame yarn worked in stockinette or reverse stockinette. Each block is 3 sts across and 4 rows high. Continue as above. Finish by machine-stitching and cutting, making sure that blocks match at both sides. There will be a seam edge on the inside of the vest so hem stitch over it with split yarn.

Finishing

Machine-stitch and cut each side and the front, making sure that the seams along the diagonal edges of the front are not too tight. Sew

down all facings.
All of the bands are worked with the solid color yarn and should be knitted more tightly than for the body of the vest (use ndls 1 or 2 sizes smaller). It is very important that the edges are not too loose. Pick up and knit sts on the sides, starting at the bottom, work up and then down again on the other side. Pick up *3 sts, skip 1*, or alternate picking up 3 and then 4. Purl back where the band meets the lower edge and then knit back (ridge). Work 6 rows stockinette and then purl 1 row on RS for fold line. Make facing the same width as band. On the 3rd row (knit), k2tog at 2 places over each shoulder (the facing should be a bit tighter here). BO loosely.
Pick up and knit sts all the way around. At the top, pick up 3 (4) sts, skip 1. Along the diagonal and back of neck, pick up 1 st in every st. Work as for the sides but at each "corner" inc/dec 2 sts on the 3rd and 5th knit rows or ridges. Also

dec 1 st at each shoulder on the 3rd knit row. Dec/inc to match on the facing.
Sew down all facings. Pin-baste the side pieces a little outside the seam for facing; try on. Sew down, placing 4-5 buttons along the edge on each side of the side pieces so that it lies flat (see photos). Sew through all the layers. Make a button loop at the front and sew on the buttons or leave open. On the model, the loops were crocheted with chain st.

Vest Buttoned at the Side

Women's/Men's

Level of Difficulty: 2

Women's Vest

Sizes	S	(M)	L	(XL)
Chest	39 ½	(41)	42 ½	(44) in
	100	(104)	108	(112) cm
Length	16 ½	(17 ¾)	18 ¼	(19) in
	42	(45)	46	(48) cm

Men's Vest

Sizes	S	(M)	L	(XL)
Chest	42 ½	(44)	46	48 in
	108	(112)	117	(122) cm
Length	22 ¾	(23 ¾)	23 ¾	(24 ½) in
	58	(60)	60	(62) cm

Lengths can be as suggested above or to desired length—see vest photos and take measurements

Yarn: Smart (100% superwash wool, 110 yds / 100 m per 50 g)
Note: The Smart yarn is slightly lighter than the tweed.

Women's: Use any color preferred. Choose a matching color for the bands or make the ridges with a contrasting color and use the vest color for the bands.

Men's: Use any tweed color you prefer. The color for the ridges should be a more muted tweed, close in shade to the MC. When working with a bold tweed, the bands should also be tweed. Alternately, you can use a Peer Gynt yarn in desired color.

Yarn Amounts
Vest in 3 colors (short):

MC	5	6	7	8 balls
CC for edging	3	3	4	4 balls
Ridge/ contrast color	1	1	1	1 ball

Vest in 2 colors (regular length):

MC	8	9	10	12 balls
Ridge/ contrast color	1	1	1	1 ball

Needles: US size 2 / 3 mm – long circular.
US size 1 / 2.5 mm circular for knitting tighter facings if desired and dpn for knitted button.
Crochet hook US size B / 2.5 mm for button.

Gauge: Solid color yarn: 24 sts and about 28-30 rows = 4 x 4 in / 10 x 10 cm.
Bold Tweed Yarn: 22 sts x about 28 rows = 4 x 4 in / 10 x 10 cm.
Adjust needle size to obtain correct gauge. The tweed yarn is slightly thicker than the solid color yarn.
Peer Gynt can substitute for tweed Smart.
Note: The same pattern and stitch count can be used for both women and men.

Notions: Pewter, plastic, horn, or leather buttons or knitted buttons for women's vest.

VEST

Women's/Men's

Knit the facing and lower section below the ridges rather tightly. With band color for women's and MC for men's, CO 200 (209) 218 (227) sts, join, being careful not to twist cast-on row. Knit 6 rnds in stockinette. On the next rnd, inc 20 (21) 22 (23) sts evenly spaced around with m1 after approx every 10th st = 220 (230) 240 (250) sts. Knit one more rnd and then purl 1 rnd on RS for fold line. You can make the fold line the same color as ridges if you want it to be more noticeable (see men's model).

Knit 6 rnds (women's) / 8 rnds (men's) in stockinette and then 1 ridge (=knit 1 rnd, purl 1 rnd) with CC; continue with MC and stockinette.

Work until piece measures (above fold line) about 8-8 ¾ in / 20-22 cm for women and 13 ¾ in / 35 cm for men or desired length to underarm. Pm at each side. BO 16 (16) 18 (18) sts centered on each underarm. CO 4 new sts over gaps for each armhole steek. Continue knitting around until armhole measures 5 ¼ (5 ¼) 5 ½ (5 ½) in / 13 (13) 14 (14) cm for women and 5 ½ (5 ½) 6 (6) in / 14 (14) 15 (15) cm for men. BO the center 2 steek sts at each side. There should now be 96 (101) 104 (109) sts for each section. BO 44 (45) 46 (47) sts at center front. Now work back and forth on the two pieces up to the neckline – 3 ½ (4) 4 ¼ (4 ¾) in / 9 (10) 11 (12) cm for women and 4 (4 ¾) 4 ¾ (4 ¾) in / 10 (12) 12 (12) cm for men. The length from the underarm should be 8 ¾ (9) 9 ¾ (10 ¼) in / 22 (23) 25 (26) cm for women and 9 ½ (10 ¼) 10 ¾ (10 ¾) in / 24 (26) 27 (27) cm for men. Wind a rubber band at the end of each needle so stitches won't fall off.

Continue working on the back for about ¾ (1 ¼) 1 ½ (2) in / 2 (3) 4 (5) cm for woman and 2 (2 ½) 2 ½ (2 ¾) in / 5 (6) 6 (7) cm for men and then BO 30 (31) 32 (33) sts at center back. Work each side separately and, at neck edge, BO 3-2-1-1 sts. Work without further shaping until back is same length as front. There should be 26 (28) 29 (31) sts for each shoulder. Join shoulders with three-needle bind-off (see Techniques).

Finishing

Side/armhole: Machine-stitch and cut down center of each side, both under and over the armhole shaping. Be careful not to cut away too much. Sew down facing, leaving an 8-in / 20-cm tail of band color. With crochet hook and MC (women's, band color), pick up and knit sts to the ridge. Continue with CC up to the armhole and then around "corner", to shoulder seam, and down the other side the same way. Alternate picking up 3 and 4 sts, skip 1 st. The last sts of the lower edge on the other side can be picked up with the MC (band) yarn tail. Make sure that you pick up 1 st at center of each "corner". You will inc/dec at each side of corner sts.

It is important that the bands be smooth and neat. If your gauge was correct, the suggestions for picking up sts above will work. If the body was knitted too tightly, then pick up fewer sts: pick up 3, skip 1 all the way around, particularly if you used the bold tweed yarn. Don't be afraid of ripping out – you don't want the bands to be too wide. Count the stitches and make sure there are the same number on each side.

Purl back to the point where you picked up sts with MC, knit back and then purl back. Now the band is worked back and forth in stockinette. As you work around, inc 1 st at each side of the center st at each "outer corner" and k2tog on each side of center st on each "inner corner." For first inc, k1f&b and then inc with m1 between these 2 sts. Purl back. Continue to inc/dec on every RS row until you've worked a total of 6 rows.

For women's vest, continue with the same color; for men's change to CC. Inc/dec only 1 time and k2tog at center of each shoulder. Knit back (fold line). Work facing to same width as band, dec and inc to match band, but omit shoulder dec. *Note:* At the shoulders, the facing will be eased in so you should dec a few sts here to prevent the band from poking out—that won't look good! On the next row, k2tog at 3 places evenly spaced over shoulder section with about 10 sts between decreases.

Men's: use CC to sew at lower edge on each side (continuation of fold line).

Neckband

With circular needle and CC, pick up and knit sts around neck. Begin at one shoulder, along the side, pick up 3 sts, skip 1; at back and front, pick 1 st in every st.

Note: Pick up 2 sts inside the edge at the sides and maintain the same width all around. This keeps the band from becoming too thick. It should lie smoothly around the neck and not poke out in some places.

The neckband should be the same width as the side bands. Dec at each "corner" 4 times. In addition, to keep the neckband smooth and rounded, work as follows:

Rnd 1: front, in each corner, work: *k2tog tbl, k1, k2tog*.

Rnd 3: Dec in each corner and at 2 places along back (towards the sides).

Rnd 5: Dec at each front corner, at each shoulder, and and 2 places on back (towards center).

Rnd 7: Dec on front in each corner, each shoulder, and 1 st at center back.

Purl 1 rnd on RS (fold line). If the

fold line is the same color as ridges, knit the 7th rnd (and the final decreases) with this color and then purl 1 rnd on RS.

Knit the facing more tightly (go down a needle size if necessary):
Rnd 1: Inc at each corner.
Rnd 2: Center front: K2tog at 2 places.
Rnd 3: Inc at each corner, at each shoulder, and 2 places along back.
Rnd 4: Knit around.

Fold down facing and make sure it is long enough to meet the band inside the pick-up row. If not, knit 1 more rnd, increasing at the corners and 2 places along back. BO loosely. The band should now lay smoothly all around the neck. Sew down facing.

Pockets with bold tweed yarn

Try on the vest and mark placement of pockets. Thread a blunt tapestry needle, insert it down into the center of a stitch on right side of pocket's bottom edge. Pull through about 11 ¾ in / 30 cm yarn. Insert a crochet hook through the st under the yarn tail. Use crochet hook to pick up this end towards the left to desired pocket width; move st to knitting needle. On our model we picked up 21 sts across. Begin knitting from the right side (where the ball of yarn is). Work to about 6 rows in stockinette less than the full length. With CC, knit 1 ridge and then 5-6 rows with MC. Knit 1 more ridge and then fold line + facing. BO. Sew down facing so it is not visible at the sides. Sew down pocket at each side.

Pockets with solid yarn

It is difficult to produce a flat seam on the RS with smooth yarn. The pockets here should be sewn on the WS.

Try on the vest and mark placement of pockets. About ¾ in / 2 cm from top edge of pocket and at the center, snip 1 st. Insert a dpn through sts below and another dpn through sts above. On the model each of the two pockets has 25 sts. Remove the knitted yarn between the two sets of sts; you can weave in those ends later. Place sts below gap on a holder. Knit the sts from upper needle to desired depth for pocket. Place sts from holder onto needle; knit 1 ridge and then band same width as neckband. Purl fold line on RS and work facing in stockinette. Sew down the band sides as smoothly as possible on RS and then sew pocket down on WS. Make a button loop at the sides for front and back buttoning (see section on sewn button loops in Techniques). Sew on buttons. Use plastic buttons in same color as MC or knit your own buttons.

Knitted Buttons

The buttons are begun with crochet and then knitted tightly on US size 1 / 2.5 mm needles. With crochet hook, ch 5, join into a ring with slip st. Ch 1 and then work 11 sc into ring. Push sc together if necessary to make room for all the stitches around; join with slip st.

With dpn, pick up 11 sts into back loops and the move last loop on crochet hook to dpn. Divide sts with 4 each on 3 dpn. Knit 2 rnds. On the next rnd, inc in each st = 24 sts. Bring the yarn to the front between the sts and knit tbl. It will be somewhat tight but it will work! Knit 1 rnd and cut yarn. Begin on another needle (to avoid holes), change color and knit 1 rnd; turn and purl 1 rnd on RS. Wrap yarn around next st and turn again. Knit 2 rnds.

On the next rnd, *K2tog, k1*, rep * to * around = 16 sts. Knit 1 rnd and bring yarn to front.

Purl and tie the 2 yarns outside the little hole. The yarn at the button center can be pulled in to hold a button. Insert a plastic ring, tighten and fasten tail. Sew through the

layers with yarn tail in the center, splitting yarn so it won't be too thick. The ring should be the same color as the yarn or slightly darker. It is possible to dye plastic rings with waterproof ink. Instead of the ring, you can use flat buttons, especially at the neck.

Roll Collar Sweater

Women's
Sweater
Cap

Level of Difficulty: 2

Sizes	S	(M)	L	(XL)
Chest	39 ½	(41 ¼)	43 ¼	(45 ¼) in
	100	(105)	110	(115) cm

Length (can be lengthened or shortened if desired)

Front	16 ½	(17 ¼)	17 ¾	(18 ¼) in
	42	(44)	45	(46) cm
Back	21	(21 ¾)	22	(22 ½) in
	53	(55)	56	(57) cm
Sleeve Length	17 ¼	(18 ¼)	19	(19) in
	44	(46)	48	(48) cm

Yarn: Smart (100% superwash wool, 110 yds / 100 m per 50 g), your choice of color + a contrast color.

Yarn Amounts
Note: The sweater can also be made without the abbreviated front. See explanation at lower left on page 94. The yarn amounts for the full length front version of the sweater are in parentheses.

Sweater				
MC	12 (14)	12 (15)	13 (15)	14 (16) balls
CC	1	1	1	1 ball

Cap (1 size): 2 balls + small amounts of contrast colors.

Needles: As needed for gauge (see Techniques) try US 3 or 4 / 3.25 or 3.5 mm—short and long circulars, dpn for sleeves and cap.

Gauge: 24 sts and approx 28 rows = 4 x 4 in / 10 x 10 cm.

Notions: small amount of fiber fill for ball at top of cap.

SWEATER
The sweater dips at the sides and the back is longer than the front. Some knitters might think that the front is too short but you can certainly knit the whole sweater in the round and make it the length you prefer. The sweater shown in the photos is particularly short.

Body
Work the lower edge in seed st. With MC, CO 55 (61) 67 (73) somewhat tightly. The knitted cast-on is rather elastic and you don't want the edge to billow out.
Sl 1, *p1, k1*, rep * to * across. CO 10 sts at end of row and then work back in seed st: sl 1, *p1, k1; rep from * across. CO 10 sts on the other side. Continue as set, casting on new sts at the beginning of the row and always slipping the first st throughout. Follow chart A for the number of sts to cast-on. Each dot = 1 purl st.
After completing all the increases (see arrow on chart), CO 45 (51) 57 (63) sts at the front = 240 (252) 264 (276) sts total. Mark the center

front st and move the marker up on each rnd; join to work in the round. Continue in seed st as shown on the chart and then stockinette until piece measures 8 ¼ (8 ¾) 9 (9) in / 21 (22) 23 (23) cm measured from bottom of front (or to desired length). Pm at each side so there are 119 (125) 131 (137) sts for the front and 121 (127) 133 (139) sts for back. BO 20 sts at each side of the body (10 sts on each side of marker).

Now work back and forth, joining a second ball of yarn so you can work on back and front at the same time to make sure they are the same length. *At the same time*, shape armholes by binding off 3-2-2-1 sts at beg of every row on front and back = 83 (89) 95 (101) sts on front and 85 (91)97 (103) sts on back. Work until piece measures 6 (6) 6 ¼ (6 ¾) in / 15 (15) 16 (17) cm from underarm. Now shape neck with short rows.

Front: Work 34 (37) 40 (43) sts; turn, sl 1, work back. Continue working short rows with 3-3-3-2-1-1 (3-3-3-2-2-1) 4-3-3-2-2-1 (4-3-3-2-2-2) sts fewer to neck edge on each RS row. Work other shoulder the same way, reversing shaping to match. There should now be 21 (23) 25 (27) sts for each shoulder. After neck shaping, work sts of each shoulder separately (place front neck sts on a holder) until total length of front is 16 ½ (17 ¼) 17 ¾ (18 ¼) in / 42 (44) 45 (46) cm. Purl the last row on RS with CC. This ridge shows both colors. Work a ridge the same way on each shoulder. Set piece aside.

Back: Work until armhole on back is 5 rows shorter than front armhole and then shape shoulders with short rows. On the next row, work 24 (26) 28 (30) sts; turn, sl 1, work back. Next work 21 (23) 25 (27); turn, sl 1, work back. Rep on other

shoulder, reversing neck shaping to match; place back neck sts on a holder.

Now join shoulders with three-needle bind-off (see Techniques) but hold pieces with WS facing WS. Begin at left shoulder, with sweater front facing you. Use CC to bind off, working from outer edge of shoulder to neck. Join right shoulders the same way but work from neck to outer edge of shoulder. Now work with sts rem from front and back necks.

Move the neck sts to a short circular. At the same time, pick up and knit 1 st at each "gap" at each side = 65 (67) 73 (79) sts on the front and 47 (49) 51 (53) sts for back = 112 (116) 124 (132) sts total.

Note: If you want the neck a bit tighter than our model, do not pick up sts in the little "holes."

You must complete the neckline before working neckband and the stitch count must the same for both parts. With the given stitch count, the neck circumference will be approx 18 ½ (19) 20 ½ (21 ¾) in / 47 (48) 52 (55) cm. If you want a neck that size, knit 2 rnds, knitting the picked-up sts tbl.

Neckband

CO the same number of sts as for neckline. It is particularly important that you use a knitted cast-on so the edge will be smooth and elastic. Work around in stockinette to desired length, about 3 ¼-6 in / 8-15 cm. End with 1 purl rnd in CC on RS (= a two-colored ridge). Now the neckband and the body can be joined.

Turn neckband inside out and place inside neckline with WS facing WS. Hold sweater so the opening with inside-out neckband faces you. Since it is worked opposite to the usual way, the three-needle bind-off will show as a stitch line on the RS. Use CC to bind-off as for shoulders.

Sleeves

The sleeves and the body are also "knitted" together with three-needle bind-off. There is no shaping for the sleeve cap. It is worked back and forth with sts at each side as for neck. The lower edge of the sleeve features a small rolled cuff.

With MC, CO 55 (55) 57 (59) sts; join and work around in stockinette for 8-10 rnds. Work the last rnd with CC. Turn work and knit 1 rnd. Turn back to RS and, with MC, knit 1 rnd and then work in seed st for about 2 in / 5 cm. Pm at center st of sleeve and end here with p1. Now begin working in seed st as a diagonal band across the sleeve over 15 sts for about 2 in / 5 cm (see chart B); the other sts are stockinette. At the same time, inc on each side of the 2 center underarm sts on every 4th rnd to a total of 103 (109) 115 (121) sts. Pin sleeve to body and try on to make sure sleeve is not too long.

Now begin working back and forth. Pm at center of underarm. Work to 5 sts from marker; turn, sl 1, work to 5 sts from other side of marker. Continue in short rows leaving, at each side, 3 sts 3 times, 2 sts 10 times, and 3 sts 2 (3) 4 (5) times; 23 sts rem at the top of sleeve. Move sts to a new needle.

Pick up and knit the same number of sts around the armhole. Use a crochet hook and MC to pick up sts and move them to a short circular. You should be able to pick up the correct number of sts by picking up 4, skipping 1. Knit 1 rnd and then, with CC, purl 1 rnd on RS (2-color ridge).

Knit the body and sleeves together as for neckband. Turn sleeve inside out and place inside body, with WS facing WS. The armhole opening should face you. Begin at the center of underarm and, with CC, work three-needle bind-off. Work the

rnds and then purl 1 rnd. Work a ridge with CC. Change to MC and knit 1 rnd.

On the next rnd, dec 8 sts evenly spaced around. Knit 6 rnds; turn and knit 7 rnds; turn and inc 8 sts evenly spaced around = 112 sts. With a smaller circular, pick up and knit sts on the lower side of CC ridge—make sure you pick up 112 sts. Knit through both layers with CC. Change to MC, purl 1 rnd on RS (2-color ridge). Now knit in stockinette with MC for about 15 rnds; if you work too many rnds here, the cap will be too long.

Crown Shaping: Make sure that decreases stack above each other. Next rnd: K10, (k2tog, k4, k2tog tbl, k20) 4 times, ending last rep with k10. There are 4 decrease lines; these "bands" of 6 sts converge at the top of the cap. Knit 4 rnds.
Next rnd: K9 (k2tog, k4, k2tog tbl, k18) 4 times, ending last rep with k9.

Knit 3 rnds.
Rep decrease rnd with 2 fewer sts between dec bands and 2 rnds between each dec rnd 1 time, with 1 rnd between dec 2 times, and then on every rnd until all sts between dec lines have been eliminated = 24 sts rem. Knit 1 rnd and then purl 1 rnd on RS (somewhat tightly). Continue knitting around for approx $5/8$-1 ¼ in / 1.5-3 cm or to desired length for "ball." K2tog around and then knit 1 rnd. Cut yarn and pull through rem 12 sts; weave in neatly on WS.

Fill ball at top with fiber fill and make a small, round patch: CO 4 sts, inc to 6 sts on next row and then dec to 4 sts on last row; BO. Sew securely inside the "ball" so it will hold the fill in place.

The brim should stand out from the cap a bit. Securely stitch the "hat band" on the inside with CC, slightly easing in upper edge. Sew with small, closely-spaced sts so the band won't be too tight for your head.

other sleeve and join the same way, making sure that you have the same number of sts as for first sleeve.

CAP

The gauge for the cap should be 24 sts in 4 in / 10 cm. You might knit the cap a little tighter than the sweater but it should not have more than 25 sts to 4 in / 10 cm.

The cap "band" is worked in 2 layers to make it thicker. It protrudes a bit and is shaped with increases and decreases.

With MC and short circular or dpn, CO 135 sts, join and work around in stockinette for approx 2 ¾ in / 7 cm.
Next rnd: *K13, k2tog; rep from * around = 126 sts.
Knit 3 rnds.
Next rnd: *K7, k2tog; rep from * around = 112 sts.
With CC, purl 1 rnd on RS and then knit 1 rnd. Change to MC and knit 1 rnd, purl 1 rnd for ridge; knit 2 rnds. Work chart C (5 rnds), knit 2

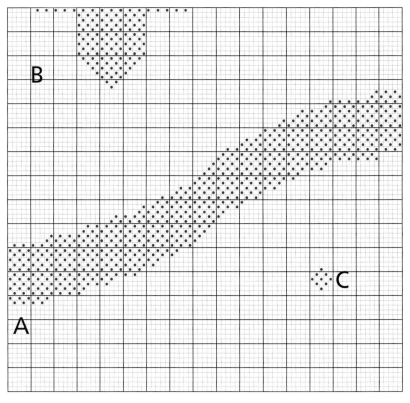

Cozy Sweater

Women's

Level of Difficulty: 2

Sizes	S	(M)	L
Chest	41 ½ in / 108 cm	(44 in / 112 cm)	46 in / 117 cm
Length, approx	19 ¾ in / 50 cm	(21 ¼ in / 54 cm)	22 ¾ in / 58 cm

Yarn
Alfa
MC: red 4063
CC: gray 1053

Yarn Amounts

MC	11 balls	12 balls	13 balls
CC	1 ball	1 ball	1 ball

Needles: Size to obtain gauge. Model shown worked with
US size 8 / 5 mm but US 9 or 10 / 5.5 or 6 mm might work better.

Gauge: 13 sts = 4 in / 10 cm (usually the gauge for this yarn is
10 sts in 4 in / 10 cm). Adjust needle size to obtain correct gauge.

Body
For this sweater, use the long-tail
cast-on and begin by working back
so that the ridge faces you.
With CC, CO 132 (138) 144 sts
with long-tail cast-on. Knit back so
that the cast-on ridge faces you.
Now join to work in the round and
change to MC. Work one rnd as
follows:
*Knit 1 st, insert right ndl under the
work, catch yarn as for a knit stitch,
knit 1 st as usual, and pass the
"caught" yarn over st just knitted*;
work * to * around. Knit the next
rnd with CC as follows: *K1, sl 1
purlwise with yarn in back; rep from
* around. Cut CC.
Now work with MC only. Purl the

CC sts and knit the MC sts of previous rnd. Knit 1 rnd and then work
in p1/k1 ribbing for one rnd with
purls over purls of previous ribbing
rnd.
From now on, knit in the round
with MC. On the first rnd, mark
sides: K1, pm, k64 (67) 70, pm, k2,
pm, k64 (67) 70, pm, k1. Knit for
4 in / 10 cm and then increase at
each side: (K1, sl marker, m1, k64
(67) 70, m1, sl marker, k1) 2 times
(= 4 sts increased on inc rnd). Work
in stockinette around for another 4
in / 10 cm and then repeat inc rnd:
(K1, sl marker, m1, k66 (69) 72, m1,
sl marker, k1) 2 times = 140 (146)
152 sts.

When piece measures 13 ½ (14 ½)
15 ¾ in / 34 (37) 40 cm or desired
length to underarm, BO 8 sts
centered at each side for armhole
and remove markers as you bind off
= 124 (130) 136 sts rem. Set body
aside while you work sleeves.

Sleeves
The first 2 rows are worked back
and forth on two needles and then
divided onto 4 dpn to work in the
round. CO 30 (32) 34 sts with CC.
Work edging as for lower edge of
body. After completing it, inc 1 st at
beg of rnd (to obtain an odd number of sts). Next, shape sleeve by
inc 2 sts centered at underarm (knit
underarm st, m1, knit around to

end of rnd and end m1) every 1 ½ in / 4 cm until there are 49 (51) 55 sts total. Continue without further shaping until sleeve measures 17 ¼ (17 ¾) 18 ¼ in / 44 (45) 46 cm or to desired length to underarm. BO 8 sts centered at underarm = 41 (43) 47 sts rem; set sleeve aside while you knit the other one the same way.

Knit 1 rnd, joining sleeves to body at underarms = 206 (216) 230 sts total. Pm at each intersection of sleeve and body for raglan seam lines (marker will be between 2 sts).

Raglan Shaping: Begin at left side of front. At each marker: k2tog tbl (or ssk) before marker and k2tog after marker = 8 sts dec per dec rnd. Dec on every other rnd a total of 8 (9) 10 times and end with 1 rnd without decreases = 142 (144) 150 sts rem. End at marker between left sleeve and left side of front.
On the next rnd, shape front shoulders: K2tog, BO 9, k24 (25) 26 (stitch counts here include the st left over from bind-off), BO 9 sts, ssk (= 10 sts eliminated at each side of front). Front now has 24 (25) 26 sts. Leave front sts on circular and work on back/sleeves only. Now work back and forth in stockinette across sleeves and back, decreasing for raglan only at back edge of each sleeve and on each side of back = 4 sts dec per dec row. On the first row only, also dec on each sleeve at front edge (to eliminate the extra st left from front shaping). Dec on back/sleeves for raglan shaping on every RS row 5 times total. On the last knit row, k20 (20) 22 sts of right sleeve, BO 10, k16 (17) 18 (including st left over from bind-off), BO 10 (= 16 (17) 18 sts rem on back) and knit rest of row. Now work back and forth over 20 (20) 22 sts of left sleeve for about 5 rows or until it reaches front neck (which has the most sts); end with yarn at back neck, cut yarn; leave

sts on circular. Work other shoulder the same way.
Round back neck with short rows: Beginning at right shoulder, k15; turn, sl 1, purl to end of row. K10, turn, sl 1, purl across. K5, turn, sl 1, knit the rest. K2, turn, 1 sl, complete row. Cut yarn. Work short rows to match on the left side of back neck. There should now be 80 (82) 88 sts and the yarn is at the back. Knit 1 row with k2tog at all the places where is a little hole where you turned rows = 8 places. The stitch count is now 72 (74) 80. Cut yarn and set piece aside.

Neckband
With CC, CO 76 (78) 84 sts and work edging as for body. Make

neckband as long as desired. Don't forget that the neck will be folded down and end with 6 rnds. For model shown neckband was worked for 4 ¾ in / 12 cm, then we decreased 4 sts evenly spaced around; turned and worked last 6 rnds.
The neckband and sweater body can now be joined with three-needle bind-off (see Techniques). With RS facing RS of neckband and sweater, knit together. If you want the ridge of the bind-off to be visible, work with WS facing WS. Seam shoulders along bound-off edges of front and back with back st (make sure seam is flexible). Sew underarm seams with back stitch.

White and Blue Cotton Tops

Level of Difficulty: 2-3

White Cotton Top

Sizes	S	(M)	L
Chest	34 ¼ in / 87 cm	(36 in / 91 cm)	37 ¾ in / 96 cm
Length	17 ¾ in / 45 cm	(19 in / 48 cm)	20 in / 51 cm

Blue Cotton Top

Chest	36 in / 91 cm	(37 ¾ in / 96 cm)	39 ¼ in / 100 cm

Yarn: Mandarin Classic (100% mercerized cotton, 120 yds / 110 m per 50 g)

Yarn Amounts

White top, tightly knit	4 balls	4-5 balls	5-6 balls
Blue top, normal gauge	4 balls	5 balls	6 balls

Needles: Size to obtain gauge. Try US size 2.5 or 4 / 3 or 3.5mm. Crochet hook for edging if desired.

Gauge: Medium gauge: 22 sts = 4 in / 10 cm; tight gauge: 24 sts = 4 in / 10 cm. Adjust needle size to obtain correct gauge.

Notions: Cotton fabric or ribbon long enough for both front bands + seam allowances. 5 plastic, mother-of-pearl or cloth buttons.

WHITE TOP, TIGHTLY KNITTED

With buttonholes on fabric bands:
Knit in the round except for the first 3 rows which are worked back and forth. With long-tail cast-on, CO 187 (195) 203 sts. Knit 3 rows back and forth = 2 ridges on RS. Join to work in the round and follow the chart, beginning at arrow for your size. Work right front and then back, beginning at arrow for your size; work left front. Continue, following the chart.
At underarm, work back and forth, following chart. If you wish to continue working in the round, add a few stitches for steeks that will be machine-stitched and cut. The back

neck shaping must be worked back and forth.
Note: If you plan on crocheting the edging for the neck and armhole bands, work the upper body back and forth.
Join shoulders with three-needle bind-off (see Techniques).

Top with knit front bands: CO 191 (201) 211 sts and work as described above, knitting 3 ridges before beginning charted rows.
Note: 4 (6) 8 sts have been added at center front and should always be knitted. They are not included on the chart.

Blue Top, Medium knitting tension

CO 201 (211) 221 sts and work as described above. Follow the chart for increased width.
Note: 4 (6) 8 sts have been added at center front and should always be knitted. They are not included on the chart.

Finishing

White Cotton Top with Fabric bands: Machine-stitch and cut at center front. Lightly steam press the pieces and try on the top. Working from WS (it's easier than working on RS), attach a strip of fabric wide enough for buttonhole/button

bands. Sew down by hand on RS or fold under and machine-stitch. The width can be adjusted at this point. Make sure the bands are completely smooth. The bands can be wider on RS than WS. Fold under to 1 knit st from patterning. Mark spacing for 5 buttonholes on right front band and make buttonholes by machine. Sew on buttons to left front band spaced as for buttonholes.

Cotton Top with Ribbon: Machine-stitch and cut at center front. Lightly steam press the pieces. Use ribbon or fabric folded as a ribbon. The ribbon is placed over the knit stitches and only a small part, about 1 stitch-width, of the WS of the knitted edge shows.
For fabric folded as a ribbon: Place fabric on WS of knitted edge so that it is folded over it and machine-stitch down. Also machine-stitch a seam to reinforce the outermost edge, just outside the fabric edge. For button loops, this edge needs to be firmer. Sew the other seams by hand. Fold under band neatly at top and bottom.
For ribbon bands: Fold the knitted edge over, pin down the ribbon, neatly fold down top and bottom and sew from front side. Sew the other seams by hand.
Make the button loops at the outermost edge. They can be crocheted or sewn (see Techniques). Sew on buttons spaced as for button loops.

Neck and Armhole Edges: Try on the top and decide how wide you want the edgings. They can be crocheted or knitted and worked to desired width. The white top shown here has crocheted edgings and the blue top features a knit edging. Make sure that the corners around the neck do not gape. Begin crochet/knitting at fabric bands.

Crocheted edgings
Begin with a row of sc on WS and

then work picot on RS. Make sure the sc row is not too tight.
The edging on our model has picot caught with a sl st plus 1 sl st. At each corner, skip a ch st between 3 slip sts.
Picot: *Ch 3, sc into first ch; 2 sl sts; rep from * across. At a few places along the back and at underarm, skip 1 ch between the 2 sl sts. The picot will then round the edges. The picot edge at lower edge of body is worked directly into the knitted edge without an initial row of sc.

Knitted edgings
Neck: Use a crochet hook to pick up sts, making sure that the edge is not too loose. Work into sts so it looks like seed st at front and back. You might need to pick up 2 sts and skip 1 at the top and into every st along diagonal lines. This might seem like too few sts but cotton stretches more in width than wool. Edging is worked back and forth. After picking up sts, knit back. On next RS: K2tog 2 times in every corner at front. On the back, K2tog

6 times evenly spaced across and 3 times at each rounded edge. Purl back.
Repeat the RS row (with decreases) and then knit back (fold line).

Facing
Knit 1 row; cut yarn and begin on other side with a new knit row. Inc 2 sts in every corner of front. Inc a total of 8 sts across back, 4 sts at each corner; purl back. BO loosely. Split yarn and use 3-4 strands to sew with. Make sure the stitches are not too long.

Armholes
Pick up sts as around neck. On size M, there should be 105 sts. Knit back. Now join and work 3 rnds: on rnds 1 and 3, k2tog evenly spaced at 2 places on each side of underarm curve = 4 sts on each rnd. Purl 1 rnd on RS (fold line). On the first knit rnd of facing k2tog at each shoulder. On rnd 2, inc 3 sts at each curve = 6 sts inc. Knit 1 rnd and then BO loosely. Sew down facings.

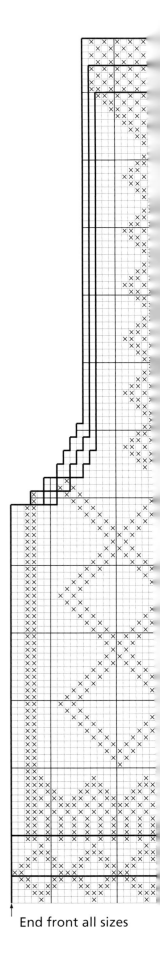

End front all sizes

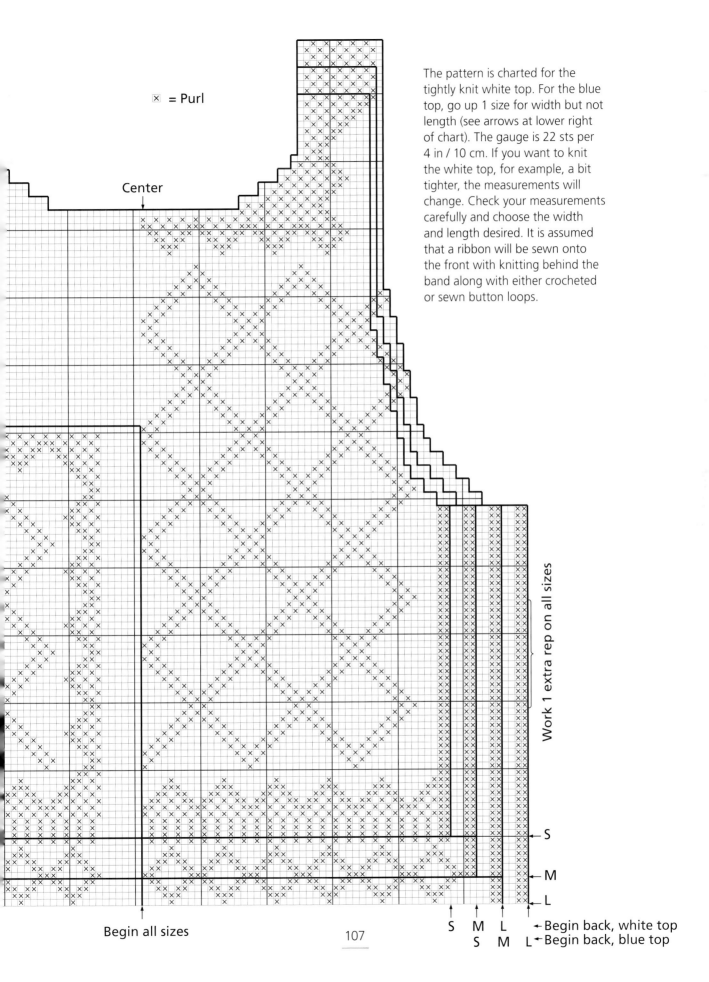

⊠ = Purl

Center

The pattern is charted for the tightly knit white top. For the blue top, go up 1 size for width but not length (see arrows at lower right of chart). The gauge is 22 sts per 4 in / 10 cm. If you want to knit the white top, for example, a bit tighter, the measurements will change. Check your measurements carefully and choose the width and length desired. It is assumed that a ribbon will be sewn onto the front with knitting behind the band along with either crocheted or sewn button loops.

Work 1 extra rep on all sizes

S

M

L

Begin all sizes

S   M   L   ← Begin back, white top
  S   M   L ← Begin back, blue top

From West Norway

Plastrons, embroidered sleeves, block panels and purl stitch patterns. Having grown up in western Norway with plastrons (a plastron is an ornamental frontispiece added to women's dress or a dress shirt front), beads and fine clothing as well as Fana jackets has made a difference to me.

The interest in these special and beautiful pattern elements with their endless possibilities has grown exponentially. In the old days, there were huge numbers of variations. Everyone made her own designs and the most diligent had the nicest clothes, of course. This multiplicity of design elements is precisely the source of renewed interest and now no one is satisfied with just two or three different versions of, for example, a plastron.

Embroidered sleeves and half-gloves were in fact very clever items. These small garments enhance any outfit (and it is easier to clean small garments rather than large ones). Half-gloves are particularly useful. They are nice and warm and make it easy to grab money and keys from pockets and small bags without removing your gloves or mittens. You'll find several examples of wrist warmers or half-gloves in this book.

Block panels are easily recognizable from the striped Fana sweaters. They were usually knitted at the lower edges of the body and sleeves. On the older, single color garments, blocks were worked with knit and purl. The blocks on the body were larger than those on the sleeves.

The first pattern knitted garments we know about were knitted with purl patterns. They were knit with wool, cotton, and silk yarn, with silk regarded as the most exclusive. It is likely that these silk garments were imported. They had eight-petal roses knitted in and could be embellished with chain st embroidery.

Wool and cotton were used for stockings, underclothes, and night clothes. Who doesn't remember handknit wool stockings and underclothes with edgings sewn onto the front and garters or stockings with small coins knitted into the holes?

Several of the garments in this book have decorative elements inspired by designs from West Norway.

JACKET WITH FRONT MOTIFS

West Norway

Women's
Jacket with or without a front motif and embroidery

Level of Difficulty: Knitting 1-2; embroidery 4-5

Sizes	S	(M)	L	(XL)
Chest	43 ¾ in / 111 cm	(46 in / 117 cm)	48 in / 122 cm	(50 ½ in / 128 cm)
Length	20 in / 51 cm	(21 in / 53 cm)	21 ¼ in / 54 cm	(22 in / 56 cm)
Sleeve length	20 ½ in / 52 cm	(21 ¼ in / 54 cm)	21 ¼ in / 54 cm	(22 in / 56 cm)

Yarn: Telemark (100% wool, 153 yds/ 140 m per 50 g (note: Telemark is no longer available)
2 colors plus yarn for embroidery. On our model, we used dark rust red 4046 and red 4118.
Note: These colors only work well together when contrasted with the embroidery colors.
If you are not going to embroider the sweater, choose different colors.

Yarn Amounts

MC	15 balls	16 balls	17 balls	18 balls
CC	2 balls	3 balls	3 balls	4 balls

Assortment of yarns and colors for embroidery.

Needles: US size 2 / 3 mm—long and short circulars + dpn; tapestry
needle for embroidery.

Gauge: 25 sts and about 29 rows = 4 x 4 in / 10 x 10 cm.
Adjust needle size to obtain correct gauge.

Notions: Buttons or brooch. On our model we used 1 medium-size
silver button from Silverfox NB.

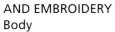

AND EMBROIDERY
Body
With MC, CO 250 (261) 272 (283) sts and join to knit in the round. Knit 30 rnds for facing. On the next rnd, inc 25 (26) 27 (28) sts evenly spaced around (after every 10th st) = 275 (287) 299 (311) sts. Knit 1 rnd and then knit picot fold line: *K2tog, yo*; rep around and end k1. Work 4 rnds k1/ p1 ribbing with purl sts over yarnovers of previous rnd, end k1. Knit 1 rnd and then purl 1 rnd on RS.

Now work panel on chart A. The blocks are knit in 2 colors and each block is 4 rnds high. On the 1st rnd, knit all sts. On the next 3 rnds, knit the CC sts and purl the MC sts. See chart: all the blocks marked with a dot are purled with MC. Work: 4 (1) 4 (1) sts with MC, *3 sts with CC, 3 sts with MC*; rep around until there are 9 (10) 10 (11) CC blocks. After the last block, knit the star (see chart). Now work 20 (21) 22 (23) blocks with CC (back). Continue with 1 star on the other front,

9 (10) 10 (11) CC blocks, then 4 (1) 4 (1) sts with MC. The 4 last sts on the round are the "steek". These sts should always be knitted with both yarns when they are in use together as: k1, p2, k1 throughout.
After the panel is complete, knit 3 rnds with MC, purl 1 rnd and knit 1 rnd. On the next rnd, inc 3 (4) 5 (6) sts evenly spaced over the 22 sts of each star (under both armholes) = 281 (295) 309 (323) sts. Knit 2 rnds, purl 1 rnd, knit 1 rnd.
Now work in knit/purl pattern fol-

lowing chart B with only MC. Over each star (25 (26) 27 (28) sts) work in stockinette all the way up. The block patterns continue from the blocks of the lower edge.

Begin chart B: K31, *p3, k3*; rep * to * to last block of lower edge. Work in stockinette at underarm and then continue with blocks on the back, stockinette at underarm, and blocks on other side of front and the last 4 sts as steek.

Continue as set until there are 12 (13) 14 (14) block repeats or to desired length to underarm. If you want to adjust the length do so at this point.

At each underarm, BO 23 (24) 25 (25) sts as well as the 2 center front steek sts. The remainder of the jacket is worked back and forth in pattern as set; always knit the first st of each row as an edge st (do not slip it). Work each section with a separate ball of yarn. Work until 1 ½ in / 4 cm from beg of neckline. End after a purl block at center front (see "Note" on chart for shaping). Follow the chart and continue with the last 36 (39) 39 (42) sts on the front and 119 (125) 131 (137) sts on the back. The last 3-4 rows are worked in stockinette. Place sts on a straight needle. From the armhole shaping there should be 16 (17) 18 (19) blocks up. On the last row of back BO the center 47 (47) 53 (53) sts and place rem sts (same number as for front) on a holder.

Join shoulders with three-needle bind-off (see Techniques). Embroider the front and lower edges of the body on each side before continuing with finishing. Embroidery: See embroidery instructions for cap and cuffs/neckband on page 116.

Sleeves (make both alike)

With CC and knitted cast-on, CO 58 (62) 66 (70) sts, join and knit 2 rnds (facing is knit after embroidery). Make picot fold line: *K2tog, yo*; rep around. Change to MC and knit 1 rnd, purl 1 rnd and then work 1 rnd with 1 st MC, 1 st CC around. End with 2 rnds MC. Work pattern border, chart D. On the 2nd rnd of pattern, inc 12 sts evenly spaced around to 70 (74) 78 (82) sts. Continue in stockinette and MC, and, *at the same time*, inc 1 st on each side of the 2 center underarm sts on every 4th rnd. Work until sleeve measures 18 ½ (19) 19 (19 ¼ in / 47 (48) 48 (49) cm or a little shorter if desired. Steam press the body and try it on. Pin on sleeves centered at sleeve shaping on body. Take into consideration that you will work for another 2 (2 ½) 2 ½ (2 ¾) in / 5 (6) 6 (7) cm. There should be 124 (130) 134 (140) sts around sleeve. If it fits, work the final 13 (14) 15 (16) rows back and forth. On the 3rd-to-last rnd work lice with CC as for lower sleeve. Purl 1 rnd, knit 1 rnd. Finish with 5 purl rows back and forth on RS for facing.

Sleeve top finishing: see Techniques. Embroider lower edges of each sleeve. See next pattern, Embroidery.

After embroidering, pick up and knit sts in cast-on row for sleeve facing. Knit 1 rnd, on the next rnd, k2tog 4 times evenly spaced around. Knit a bit tighter than the panel so that the facing doesn't gape. Make facing long enough to cover panel and then BO. Embroider a row of chain st or stem stitch around the lower edge, inserting needle slightly into bottom layer so that the edge is held in place.

Finishing

Machine-stitch and cut at center front. Sew down lower facing on body. Knit back and forth around the edge. Begin at lower edge of front on the right side of jacket. With CC, pick/knit up sts all the way around, pick up *3-4 sts, skip 1 st*. Along the "diagonal" and back, pick up 1 st for every st. Knit back (= 1 ridge). On the next work, work dots, 1 st with MC and 1 st with CC; purl back.

On the next 2 RS rows, inc 1 st in the "outward curves" and dec 1 st at the "inward curves." *At the same time*, on the last knit row, k2tog at back neck on each side of the 3 center sts.

Work fold line (1 purl row on RS) and facing. On the facing, inc and dec to match RS. Make facing same width as edging and BO purlwise on RS.

Pin facing in place and sew down lightly to edge at front. Sew down front facing with split yarn (see Techniques), working through both lower layers.

Now make a lining for the front. CO 31 sts and work back and forth in stockinette. This lining goes from the point where the fold line was sewn down and up along the front. Follow the edge and dec as on front. Continue up to the shoulder joining. Lightly steam press and sew down lining all around. Attach sleeves with RS facing along the first purl row.

JACKET WITHOUT FRONT MOTIF AND EMBROIDERY

Work as described above but also make the block effect in the front. See chart and find which block is lowest at front. Continue as described.

You might want to add a narrow stripe with CC at the top of both the body and sleeves (see jacket in photo on page 110).

Sleeves

The facing doesn't need to be as wide as described above. If you'd like embroidery here, follow the explanations.

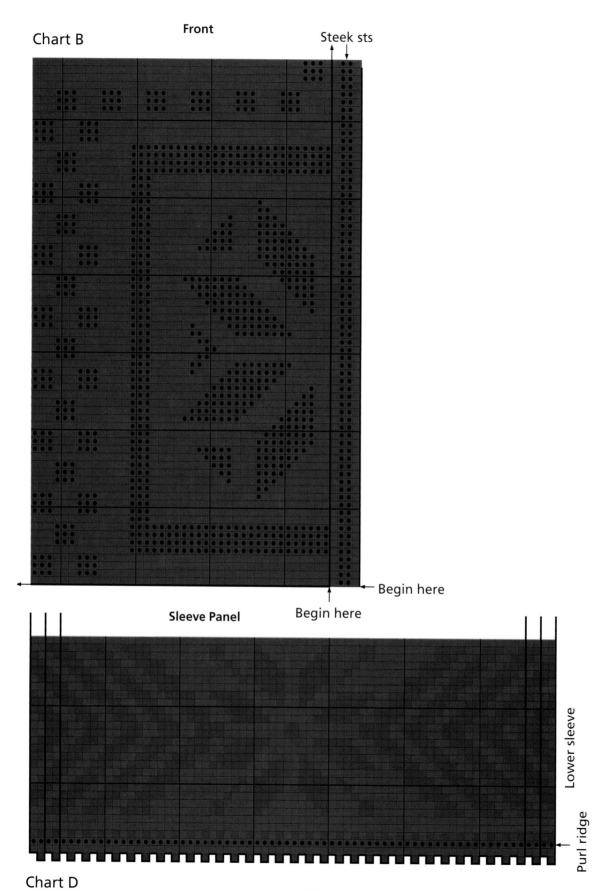

Chart B

Front

Steek sts

← Begin here

Begin here

Sleeve Panel

Lower sleeve

Purl ridge

Chart D

Lower Panel

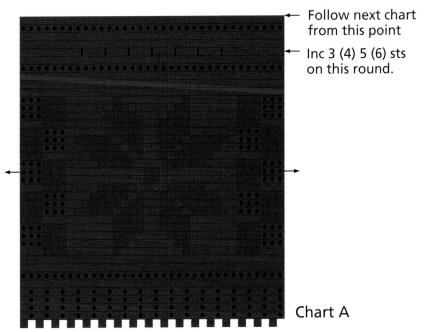

← Follow next chart from this point

← Inc 3 (4) 5 (6) sts on this round.

Chart A

Chart C

Front Shaping

Note (see text)

Steek sts

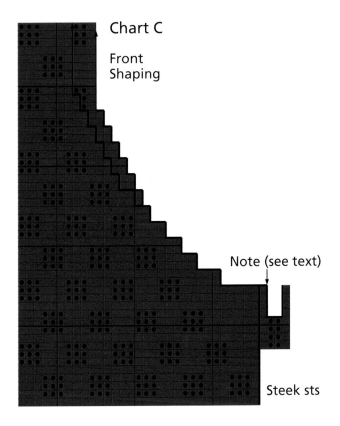

Cap and Wrist/Neck Warmers

Cap
Wrist Warmers/Neck Warmer

Level of Difficulty: 4-5

Yarn
Telemark (100% wool, 153 yds / 140 m per 50 g (note: Telemark is no longer available): MC: white 1012; CC: red 4265, black 1099, pink 4745

Yarn Amounts
Wrist Warmers: 1 ball of each color
Cap (1 size): 1 ball of each color
For both pieces: 2 balls white and 1 ball red + small amounts of the other colors for the borders and embroidery.

Needles: US size 1.5 / 2.5 mm — short circular and set of 5 dpn.

Notions: 6 Silverfox (or other small silver or pewter) buttons, NB 5 small.

CAP
The cap should be knitted somewhat tightly: 26 sts = 4 in / 10 cm. With MC, CO 128 sts; join, being careful not to twist cast-on row. Work in stockinette for about 3 ¼-4 ¾ in / 8-12 cm or to desired length of rolled edge. Work panel on chart A. On the last rnd of the first ridge, dec 1 st and, on the last rnd of the last ridge, dec 1 = 126 sts rem. After completing panel, with MC, knit 2 rnds. On the next rnd, dec 6 sts evenly spaced around: *k19, k2tog*; rep * to * around = 120 sts rem. Now begin top shaping:
Rnd 1: *K10, k2tog*; rep * to * around. Knit 3 rnds.
Rnd 4: *K9, k2tog*; rep * to * around. Knit 2 rnds.

Now decrease on every other rnd, with 1 less st between decreases, until 10 sts rem. Cut yarn, pull through rem sts, pull tight, and neatly weave in tail on WS.

WRIST WARMERS/ NECKWARMER
Worked in the round with 4 dpn. If you prefer to knit back and forth, CO 1 less st. There is 1 extra st on each side of the piece so that you can pick up sts later.
It isn't necessary to twist strands around each other because the pieces will be embroidered and a facing covers the WS. This makes the pieces smoother.
With CC3, CO 55 (= 52 charted sts + 3 for steek) sts. Change to

CC2 and knit 1 ridge (see arrow on chart). The section below the ridge will be knit later.
Now work chart B. The last 3 sts of the round are the steek sts. Knit these sts with both strands when working in color pattern.
Make the picot edging with the same color as the ridge (it makes small points along the edge):
K1, *yo, k2tog*; rep * to * around. Knit 2 more rnds and then change to MC. At the same time, dec 8 sts evenly spaced around. Knit half of the facing (about 10 rnds) and then BO loosely. Weave in the tail so that it won't be in the way when you pick up sts at the sides for the buttons and loops. Make the other wrist warmer mirror image.

Machine-stitch and cut steek (see Techniques). Work embroidery before completing finishing.

Embroidery

Split the yarn for chain and stem st but not for daisy and V-stitches. You can choose another yarn for the embroidery (for example, if needed for contrast colors) but it should be the same quality and thickness as the garment yarn. We've used a deep rose for our models.

The embroidery will be easier and more even if you embroider the same motif on each cuff and the cap before working on a different motif. Begin with the largest motif and then work on the details. Each motif is surrounded with chain and stem st, stitched in opposite directions. To keep the work smooth, *do not stitch between knit sts*. If you do, the stitches will be uneven and pull in. If it is difficult to embroider straight lines, you can insert the needle a tiny bit into the previous st. Make sure the embroidery is neither too loose nor too tight and hold the thread when turning. Embroider the outermost chain stitches first so that they cover the shift between the two colors. The direction of the stitches is not very important when using a dark yarn but a good method for working is to begin at the center and stitch to the right on the right side of the motif and towards the left on the left side. The inner seam(s) are stem st embroidered closely to the outermost line. Make short stem sts so that the seam is somewhat tight.

The color changes in the knitting should be covered as well as possible so the overall look is clean and neat. Insert the needle into the yarn and not between stitches. Be careful about the stitch direction. On a matching set of cap and wrist warmers, 2 lines/colors are sewn with stem st inside each rose petal, towards the right with one color and leftwards with the other; reverse on the other side of the rose. Insert the yarn down into each "petal" and up again so that the points are distinctive.

Instead of the two stem st lines, you can make 1 row of chain st. This makes the pattern more open but it is also easier.

Make a daisy st in the center of the rose, 8 petals with 2 colors. Work the details as you choose.

V-stitch is sewn around "the root" of each daisy chain petal (see picture).

Beads can be sewn on with sewing thread in the same color as beads, 3 sts in each bead.

Instead of beads you can make small knots or crosses.

When the embroidery is complete, finish the back of the piece.

Pick up sts directly into the cast-on row, knit 1 rnd or, if you have already cut the steek open, work back and forth.

Continue with the picot edging, decreases and remainder of the facing (about 10 rows) as for the first side. The sides of the facing meet at the center; sew them together with fine sts so the seam will be elastic. Machine-stitch and cut steeks.

After the facing has been joined, embroider along the picot edging, going down into the facing when making these sts.

With a crochet hook and a small size knitting needle, pick up about 20 sts with same color as ridges on each side for the button and button loop bands. Pick up sts through both layers – pin layers together so they won't slide. Knit back, 1 ridge, and then 2 rows stockinette. The edge should be as narrow as possible. Make sure that it isn't "wavy." Purl 1 row on RS for fold line and then make facing same width as band. Sew down facing. Make 3 button loops on the side with the large star, each over 2 strands of yarn (see Techniques). Try on the wrist warmers and then sew on buttons. If you button the cuffs together you can wear them as a neckwarmer.

Chain St

"Daisy" St

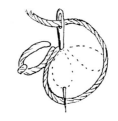

Right- and Left-leaning Stem St

Cap Panel

Chart A

1 ridge →

1 ridge →

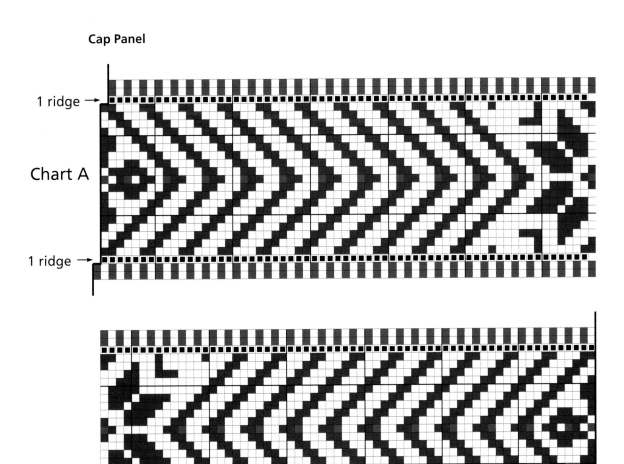

Chart B

1 ridge →

1 ridge →

← Picot Edging

← Cast-on
← Picot Edging

+3 Steek sts

117

Suppliers

Halcyon Yarn
12 School Street
Bath, ME 04530
800-341-0282
www.halcyonyarn.com
service@halcyonyarn.com

Webs—America's Yarn Store
75 Service Center Road
Northampton, MA 01060
800-367-9327
www.yarn.com
customerservice@yarn.com

Importing and Offering Norwegian Yarns, Pewter Buttons and Clasps, Knitting Accessories

Nordic Fiber Arts
4 Cutts Road
Durham, NH 03824-3101
603-868-1196
www.nordicfiberarts.com
info@nordicfiberarts.com

For help choosing a suitable yarn substitution contact one of the suppliers above or your local yarn shop for help. There are numerous yarn suppliers and useful information that can be found on the internet.

Norwegian sources for the silver buttons / clasps:

Hasla Setesdalsylv AS
B-4747 Valle i Setesdal
setsylv@online.no
www.setesdalsylv.no

Kirsten Bråten Berg
Bergsam AS
www.bergsam.no